OUTLAWS
LAWMEN of Western Canada

Volume Three

Constable Edgar Millen who was killed by the Mad Trapper on the Rat River, January 30, 1932.

Copyright © 1987, 2000 Heritage House Publishing Co. Ltd
CANADIAN CATALOGUING IN PUBLICATION DATA

Main entry under title:

Outlaws and lawmen of western Canada

ISBN 1-895811-79-1 (v. 1). —ISBN 1-895811-85-6 (v.2).
—ISBN 1-89811-87-2 (v. 3)

    1. Outlaws—Canada, Western—History. 2. Criminals—Canada,
Western—History. 3. Police—Canada, Western—History.

FC3217.1.A1098   1999   364.1'092'2712   C99-910257-5
F1060.3.098   1999

Printing History: First edition – 1987
                     Reprinted – 2001

Heritage House acknowledges the financial support of the Government of
Canada through the Book Publishing Industry Development Program (BPIDP)
for our publishing activities. Heritage House also acknowledges the support
of the British Columbia Arts Council and the British Columbia Archives.

Front cover: A North-West Mounted Policeman rides into an Indian
encampment to arrest a suspect. The painting is by famed Western artist Charles
M. Russell (1864-1926) who used Western Canada and the Mounties as the
theme for many paintings. Courtesy Buffalo Bill Historical Center, Cody,
Wyoming.

HERITAGE HOUSE PUBLISHING COMPANY LTD.
Unit #108 - 17655 66 A Ave., Surrey, B.C. V3S 2A7

Printed in Canada

Photo Credits
British Columbia Archives: 36-37, 41, 45, 50; Canadian Department of Energy,
Mines and Resources: 22; Glenbow Archives: 11, 22, 23, 26, 27, 30, 32, 33,
90, 91-92, 93, 95, 100, 103, 105, 107, 111; Godsell, P.H.: 84, 85; Heritage
House: 48, 51, 55, 100, 114; Manitoba Archives: 29; Montana Historical
Society: 48; National Museum of Canada: 79; Provincial Archives of Alberta:
58-59, back cover; Public Archives of Canada: 120, 122, 123, 128; RCMP:
11, 13, 16, 22, 26, 30, 66, 68, 78-79, 82, 88, 107, 116-117, 118; Saskatchewan
Archives Board: 68, 75; Vancouver City Policy: 144; Vancouver Public
Library: 140, 144; Western Canada Pictorial Index: 148, 156.

Canada

CONTENTS

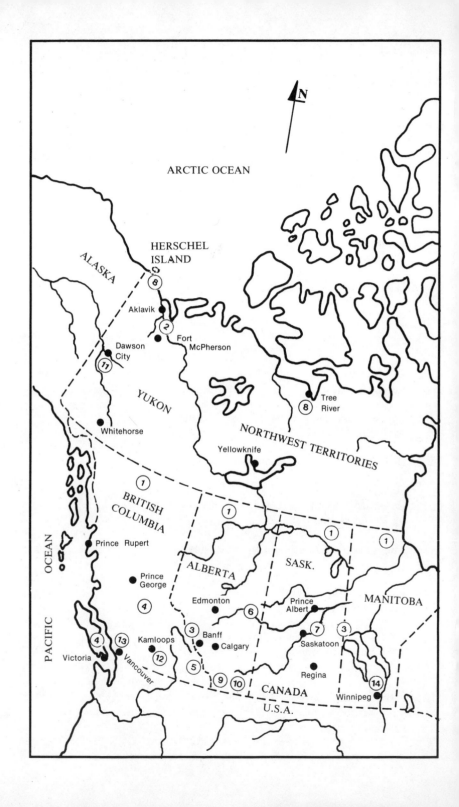

Western Canada's First Police Forces

B.C. PROVINCIAL POLICE

These lawmen were the first in Western Canada, their heritage dating to November 19, 1858, when the Crown Colony of British Columbia was established. Chartres Brew of the Irish Constabulary was appointed Chief Inspector of Police, his task formidable. That summer some 30,000 men had stampeded to a gold discovery on the Fraser River. They were mostly from the U.S., all armed with a six-gun, sometimes two, a rifle and a Bowie knife. To maintain order Brew began with about a dozen men to police a wilderness region that didn't have a mile of road.

Larger than California, Oregon and Washington combined, it extended some 500 miles (800 km) from the Pacific Ocean east to the Rocky Mountains, and 1,000 miles (1,600 km) from the U.S. border to what would one day become the Yukon. During the frontier era the new lawmen patrolled by canoe and horseback in summer, dog team and snowshoes in winter. There are many instances of them bringing prisoners over 500 miles (800 km) by horseback, stagecoach and canoe to a courtroom. In addition, they had to be adept with tiller and mainsail since they also patrolled some 5,000 miles (8,000 km) of coastline.

As historian H.H. Bancroft wrote: "Never in the pacification and settlement of any section of America have there been so few disturbances, so few crimes against law and order."

They were to serve for almost a century — from 1858 until 1950 when they were absorbed into the RCMP. Of them, Deputy Commissioner Cecil Clark wrote in Heritage House book, *B.C. Provincial Police Stories*:

"These far-ranging police officers saw not only the coming of the telegraph, the telephone and electric light but also were on duty when the four-horse stagecoach gave way to the train, the automobile and the airplane. They readily embraced anything new that would make them more efficient and were proud that their experiments enabled them to establish the first city-to-city, short-wave police radio communication system in North America.

"Whether assisting victims of fire or flood or merely performing the daily routine of urban duty, these British Columbia policemen did it with pride born of a sense of history. Thirteen died in the performance of their duty, expecting nothing more than that they be remembered."

MANITOBA PROVINCIAL POLICE

The Manitoba Provincial Police was formed in October 1870 soon after Manitoba became the first province in Western Canada. It consisted of nineteen men, under Captain John Villiers, with a miscellany of weapons and an odd assortment of uniforms. After two years the force had shrunk to eight. Among the few remaining was Richard Power who joined the original force when he was nineteen. In February 1874 at twenty-three he became Chief Constable, probably the youngest man in Canada to hold this position.

He quickly established a reputation for courage and for toting a huge Colt .45 with a nine-inch barrel. He also became the first Chief Constable to die on duty. On July 28, 1880, he was escorting an escaped convict named Mike Carroll back to jail when Carroll deliberately upset a rowboat that was to take them across the Red River. Both were drowned.

Over the years as the population increased so did the police force. But as in all other Western provinces the officers were few in number, their territory massive. In addition, funds were always skimpy, a situation aggravated by the depression of the early 1930s. Finally, the province decided that it couldn't afford its own police force. As in Saskatchewan, Alberta, New Brunswick, Nova Scotia and Prince Edward Island, the RCMP took over police duties. The Manitoba Provincial Police became history.

SASKATCHEWAN PROVINCIAL POLICE
As noted on page 72, the Saskatchewan Provincial Police was born under shaky circumstances on January 1, 1917. But within two years Commissioner C.A. Mahoney was able to report that 106 men were on staff. Sixty-two of these were ex-RNWMP and another twenty-four had experience in police forces throughout the world. He had quickly welded together a force that was professional and had strong pride in itself.

But like all other Western Canadian forces, it was not destined to survive. In November 1926 Saskatchewan Premier James G. Gardiner wrote to the Federal Minister of Justice pointing out that an impossible situation existed with regard to policing the province.

"We have a condition which developed during the war, which leaves us with virtually three police forces, the RCMP, the Provincial Police and the Municipal Police," he noted. "The result is that there is overlapping ... and cost which, if continued, will develop a first class political issue.

As a result of Premier Gardiner's letter, on June 1, 1928, the Federal government again took over police duties. About 50 of the 140 men in the provincial force were absorbed into the RCMP. But for the others, as author F.W. Anderson noted:

"... it was the careful setting on a shelf of a travel-stained Stetson hat with the brim turned up on the left; the fond fingering of a shoulder insignia or a badge carefully preserved. Probably none of them realized that their exploits would be so quickly forgotten; their discreet but thorough handling of a thousand minor offences and grievances so soon unappreciated; and their quiet heroism in the face of danger passed over."

ALBERTA PROVINCIAL POLICE
Like neighboring Saskatchewan, the Alberta force was formed in 1917 when the RNWMP withdrew from the province. The main burden of organizing the force was thrust on its new Deputy Chief, John D. Nicholson, who had retired from the RNWMP after a distinguished career. As he later noted: "The organization of the Alberta Provincial Police took place in my office and the first 100 men were sworn in by myself."

The main problem confronting the new lawmen was enforcing prohibition. It was a distasteful task to the policemen and more so to many citizens, especially in Southern Alberta where residents had voted against prohibition. As a consequence, in the Crowsnest Pass region bootlegging flourished. For instance, on July 24, 1920, some seventy couples assembled at the Opera House in Blairmore. The attraction wasn't opera but the annual ball of the Pass Bootleggers' Association. As the local paper noted: "Representatives of almost every bootleg joint in the Pass were present."

The light-hearted approach, however, was an illusion. Bootlegging had deadly undertones as indicated by the articles on pages 90 and 102. To help combat the bootleggers, in 1923 the Alberta Provincial Police force added six motorcycles to improve enforcement. Two of the bikes had mounted machine guns and, as shown on the back cover, the other four had sidecars equipped with submachine guns.

Open warfare loomed but on November 5, 1923, Albertans voted to end prohibition. The so-called "dry era" had lasted eight years and cost the lives of four police officers.

The Alberta Provincials continued to serve until 1932 when economic conditions resulted in the RCMP taking over. Although they never numbered over 125, they wrote a proud record. Unfortunately, as in most other provinces, little has been done to commemorate their dedicated service.

NORTH-WEST MOUNTED POLICE

This force, today's RCMP, was born in 1873 when the 1,000-mile (1,600-km) region between Manitoba and the Rocky Mountains was a wilderness called the North-West Territories. It was a lawless land where U.S. whiskey traders were rapidly wiping out the Blackfoot, Cree and other Plains tribes.

Wrote the Reverend John McDougall, one of the West's renowned missionaries: "Scores of thousands of buffalo robes and hundreds of thousands of wolf and fox skins and most of the best horses the Indians had were taken south into Montana, and the chief article of barter for these was alcohol. In this traffic very many Indians were killed, and also quite a number of white men. Within a few miles of us...forty-two able bodied men were the victims among themselves, all slain in the drunken rows. These were Blackfoot.... There was no law but might. Some terrible scenes occurred when whole camps went on the spree, as was frequently the case, shooting, stabbing, killing, freezing, dying.

"Thus these atrocious debauches were continuing all that winter not far from us. Mothers lost their children. These were either frozen to death or devoured by the myriad dogs of the camp. The birth-rate decreased and the poor red man was in a fair way towards extinction...."

The alcohol with which the traders were fleecing the Indians of their robes, horses and other possessions — including women — was a terrible concoction. Each trader brewed his own, the motive to maximize profits.

"I never knowed what made an Injun so crazy when he drank till I tried this booze...." wrote cowboy author-artist Charles M. Russell, one of whose paintings is on the cover. "You could even shoot a man through the brain or heart and he wouldn't die till he sobered up."

Stamping out this whiskey trade was the prime reason for the forming of the new police force. Recruiting began in September 1873 and since most newcomers couldn't ride a horse, training continued all winter at Lower Fort Garry and Toronto. In the summer of 1874 the force was assembled at Dufferin, Manitoba, resplendent in scarlet Norfolk jacket, steel grey breeches or blue trousers with a double blue stripe and a pill-box hat that proved useless. Their rifles were about the same. They were single-shot, although both the Indians and whiskey traders were armed with Winchester or Henry repeating rifles.

On June 8, 275 officers and men began a trek some 800 miles (1,290 km) to within sight of the Rocky Mountains. Since the force had to be self-supporting once it reached the plains the cavalcade included 310 horses, over 200 head of cattle, 114 Red River carts, 73 wagons, ploughs, mowers, and other farming implements. Two unwieldy cannon weighing over a ton each were also dragged along because the commanding officer, G.A. French, expected "hot work" when they arrived.

The whiskey traders, rumored to number 500, had established a series of forts in what is today southern Alberta. The largest was Fort Whoop-Up which took thirty men two years to construct. Built of squared timbers, it had palisades, loopholes for rifles and two bastions complete with cannon.

On October 9 the force reached Fort Whoop-Up after a hectic trek which had taken four months and during which men and horses had suffered greatly, with many animals dying of starvation. As Sub-Constable E.H. Maunsell wrote:

"Although it was fortunate that we had buffalo meat to eat, being out of provisions, still straight boiled meat soon palled on the palate. We were all attacked with diarrhea, which greatly weakened us. Not only did we eat boiled buffalo meat, using their dried dung for fuel, but on occasions were forced to drink diluted buffalo urine."

But instead of "hot work" at the fort they found it abandoned except for a bearded trader named Dave Akers and his Indian "wife." (An old-timer credited Akers with purchasing forty Indian women as "wives" during his years on the plains.) So well constructed was Fort Whoop-Up that Colonel Macleod offered to buy it as a headquarters for $10,000. Akers wanted $25,000. The price was too high for Macleod and, led by guide Jerry Potts, the force headed northwest 60 miles (100 km) to the Oldman River where they built Fort Macleod, the first NWMP post in Western Canada.

But Macleod didn't wait for the fort to be finished before starting after the whiskey traders. Within a few days they made the first arrests. All that winter in blizzards and sub-zero weather the pursuit continued. In a few months law and order prevailed, but not without cost. On October 26 Constable Godfrey Park died of typhoid and was the first man buried in Fort Macleod cemetery. In December Constables Baxter and Wilson were caught in a blizzard while on patrol and froze to death.

In 1875 the policemen established a second post which they named Fort Calgary, better known today as Alberta's second largest city, Calgary. During subsequent years their duties included maintaining law and order among thousands of workers during construction of the Canadian Pacific Railway in the early 1880s. Then in the 1890s they were responsible for the hundreds of thousands of settlers flooding the West — an influx summarized by one Indian as: "The plains were black with white men." Many of the settlers had never been out of the city; many more could not speak English. To help safeguard them every settler was regularly visited by a policeman.

The area covered by horseback and buggy was huge. In one year out of Regina alone, patrols travelled some 350,000 miles (560,000 km).

In 1890 the NWMP were given another massive responsibility — Arctic Canada. The first force of nineteen men arrived in the Yukon in 1895 and when the discovery of gold in 1896 resulted in 50,000 men stampeding North, the Mounties upheld their motto "Maintain the Right."

In the history of the force there are many instances of a few policemen — at times single handedly, as artist Charles M. Russell portrays on the cover — maintaining law and order. In 1876, for instance, the Sioux Indians made their way to Canada after wiping out Lieutenant Colonel George A. Custer and over 200 of his cavalrymen.

The first group of some 2,000 arrived late in 1876, many proudly carrying the scalps of Custer's cavalrymen. They were met by Superintendent J.M. Walsh with twelve men. He informed their chief, Black Moon, that the laws of Canada had to be obeyed or the Indians would be sent back. He didn't explain, however, how his twelve policemen would accomplish the task, especially since the Indians were well armed with guns from the dead soldiers. Although there would be many tense confrontations between the red men and the red-coated Mounties, there were no deaths. Eventually American and Canadian negotiators persuaded the Sioux to return to their reservations in the U.S.

In the book, *The Pictorial History of the Royal Canadian Mounted Police*, the force's historian, S.W. Horrall, recounts another of the many instances of "single handed" law enforcement:

"In 1883, a band of Cree under Piapot pitched their camp on the C.P.R. right-of-way. Corporal Wilde and a constable from Maple Creek were sent to investigate. Wilde's demand that they move was greeted with defiance and ridicule. The Indians refused and tried to provoke the two policemen by jostling them and discharging firearms. It was a challenge to authority; to retreat would have resulted in a loss of face. Wilde decided to take the upper hand. Coolly producing his pocket watch, he announced that he would give the Indians fifteen minutes to comply with his order to move. When the time was up, he dismounted, strode over to Piapot's lodge and began dismantling it. Faced with Wilde's bold action the Indians backed down."

In October 1896 Sergeant Wilde was murdered in another single-handed operation. He was chasing an Indian fugitive called Charcoal on horseback. Sergeant Wilde's big horse, Major, was rapidly closing on the fleeing Indian and Wilde could easily have shot him. Instead he rode up alongside and leaned forward to yank Charcoal from his saddle. There was a muffled report and the tall figure of the Mountie hurtled to the snow.

Charcoal was later caught and hanged. Sergeant Wilde was buried at Fort Macleod, joining the growing number of crosses marking men who had died on duty.

In 1904 as a reward for the dedicated service performed by the North-West Mounted Police, King Edward VII conferred the prefix "Royal" to their name. Then in 1920 there was another name change. The Royal North-West Mounted Police became today's familiar Royal Canadian Mounted Police. Speeding ticket, anyone?

He was a loner, a deadly shot who in 1932 triggered the greatest manhunt in the history of Arctic Canada. Over half a century later the mystery remains — who was the

Mad Trapper
of Rat River

The Savage rifle with which Johnson killed Constable Edgar Millen and seriously wounded Constable A. King, opposite page, and Staff Sergeant H. Hersey. The rifle and Johnson's other effects are on display in the RCMP Museum at Regina.

Albert Johnson, far right, after being shot to death on the Eagle River.

A stranger arrived at Ross River Post, Yukon Territory, August 21, 1927, and made his way to Taylor and Drury's Trading Store. Although not too much information was volunteered, trader Roy Buttle learned that the newcomer's name was Arthur Nelson, that he was a trapper, and that he intended to stay just long enough to build a boat.

The storekeeper said he would lend a hand and Nelson, although not too enthusiastic at first, finally accepted the offer. In view of the fact that Buttle did not outwardly show much curiosity or ask too many questions, the reticent Nelson did confide a few things to Buttle over the nine days it took them to build the boat.

Roy Buttle found Nelson intelligent and detected something in the man's make-up that made him seem odd. For one thing, Buttle was the only person around the Post the trapper would have anything to do with. He camped about half a mile from the settlement and openly showed that he welcomed no guests. Also, the Indians living around the Post were visibly afraid of the stranger and would have absolutely nothing to do with him.

This was not because Arthur Nelson was a towering giant of a man. Of average height, his well-proportioned frame packed about 177 pounds (77 kg). His speech carried a trace of Scandinavian and he walked with an habitual stoop as if he had been used to carrying a heavy shoulder pack.

When the boat was finished, Nelson left the Post on August 30, travelling up river. He returned to Ross River the following June and stayed for a month until the trading store's annual supply boat arrived. He told Roy Buttle he had been trapping at Ross Lake during the winter. After the supplies came in, Nelson purchased a few provisions, a Savage .30-.30 carbine and some .22 shells. He left without warning in mid-July.

About a month later three trappers, Oley Johnson, Norman Niddery and Oscar Erickson, were travelling up the south fork of the Stewart River. One morning as they were eating breakfast at Twin Falls, a stranger approached them. They invited him to join them, but he refused, saying he

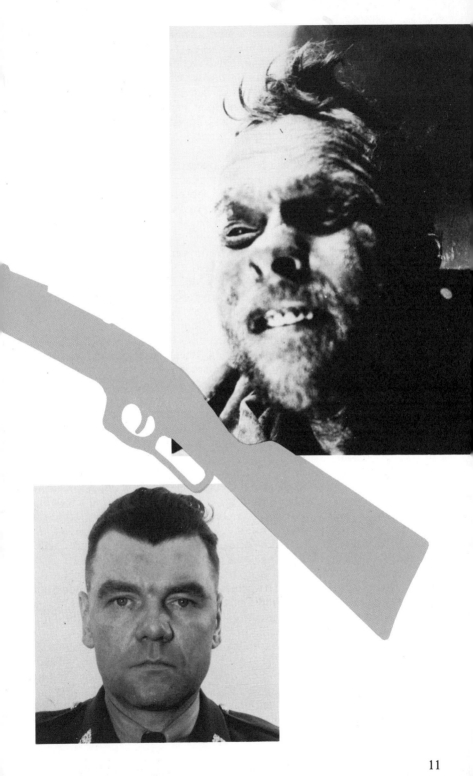

had camped overnight upstream a piece and had already eaten. He told them his name was Arthur Nelson and asked the way to Keno, Y.T. After learning the way, he hiked off in that direction.

Robert Levac who operated a trading store at Fraser Falls was the next man to come into contact with Nelson. The latter asked if he could stop over a day or two and Levac put him up in a spare cabin. Nelson wanted to get rid of some marten skins he had trapped, but Levac wouldn't buy them. He said he would bid on them, but suggested that Nelson take them to Mayo, Y.T., to sell.

A few days later, Arthur Nelson appeared in Mayo. One of the first things he did was to peddle his marten skins at the Taylor and Drury Store for $680. This transaction was completed between Nelson and W.H. Jeffrey of the firm on August 30, 1928. Nelson received this amount in cash through an arrangement between Taylor and Drury and the Bank of Montreal in Mayo, as the store did not have that much cash on hand.

The next two winters Nelson spent trapping in the Macmillan River district between Ross River Post and Mayo. On two occasions he visited the trading store at Russell Creek run by Mr. Zimmerlee. Although Zimmerlee did not see Nelson carrying firearms at any time, the trapper asked for some shotgun shells on one occasion when he purchased supplies at the store.

In the spring of 1931, trapper P. Frederickson of the Russell Post area sold a canoe to Nelson who paddled up the Macmillan River, and later some Indians in the district found the canoe abandoned on the upper waters of that river. Nelson returned to Mayo shortly after leaving the Macmillan River area, stopping off long enough to pick up a few provisions, including an abundant quantity of kidney pills. Clerk Archie Currie of Binet's Store was rather startled when Nelson bought six boxes of pills, but Nelson was so uncommunicative that Currie thought twice about engaging the man in any conversation.

In May 1931, Arthur Nelson headed north to Keno. He stopped there briefly, making a small purchase in the store then began walking north again. Frank Gillespie was having a cup of tea at the mouth of Crystal Creek one morning when Nelson happened upon his campfire. Gillespie offered the traveller a cup, but Nelson refused, asking where the bridge on the McQuesten River was located as he said he was going to Haggart Creek. At the time, Nelson was laboring under the weight of a heavy shoulder pack.

"Snoose" Erickson and his partner, Sullivan, had a cabin on the McQuesten River in May 1931 when Nelson passed that way at noon one day carrying the heavy pack and a small rifle. Erickson asked the stranger to have lunch with them, but he curtly refused and kept walking in the direction of eight-mile cabin near the head of the Beaver River.

From the head of the Beaver River, Yukon Territory, in May 1931, trapper Arthur Nelson seemingly vanished just as strangely as he had suddenly appeared at Ross River Post nearly four years earlier. But had he vanished?

On July 9, 1931, a stranger arrived at Fort McPherson, North-West Territories, under rather unusual circumstances. This man drifted down the Peel River from the direction of the Yukon Territory on a raft con-

Staff Sergeant H. Hersey, above, who was wounded in the final gun battle. Constable McDowell, above right, mushed 80 miles (130 km) in a record twenty hours getting Constable King to Aklavik.

Dr. J. Urquhart, wearing glasses below, saved the lives of Constable King and Staff Sergeant Hersey during the Johnson chase. Also in the photo is Mrs. Urquhart and, at right beside her, Inspector A. Eames who directed the pursuit.

structed of three large logs to a spot about 3 miles (5 km) above Fort McPherson. There he abandoned his crude craft and apparently with little or no outfit, walked the rest of the way into the Fort where he purchased supplies. He was said to be well stocked with cash.

This information was passed along to Inspector Alexander Neville Eames who commanded the Western Arctic Sub-District of the Royal Canadian Mounted Police with headquarters at Aklavik, N.W.T. Constable Edgar Millen, in charge of the Force's Detachment at Arctic Red River, was sent instructions to interview the stranger.

Constable Millen located the newcomer in Fort McPherson on July 21 where he was purchasing more supplies. He told the policeman his name was Albert Johnson, that he had come into the country via the Mackenzie River and that he had spent the previous year on the prairies. Asked about his plans, he said he was undecided, but had considered going over the Rat (River) portage. He told Constable Millen he would not live in the settlement as he did not want to be bothered with anyone and wished to live entirely alone. The policeman was aware that Johnson did not wish to divulge much in the way of information about himself.

Constable Millen later learned from Northern Traders Ltd. and the Hudson's Bay Company that Johnson was definitely getting an outfit together for a trip over the Rat portage. On the next patrol to Fort McPherson in August Constable Ronald Melville found that Albert Johnson left the settlement on July 28, paddling down river in a canoe he had purchased from an Indian. The policeman learned from Arthur N. Blake, who lived at the mouth of the Husky River, that Johnson passed his place looking for the Rat River, but had apparently missed it, because a few days later he returned and stopped at Blake's home.

Johnson told Blake that he was going into the Yukon Territory and not returning. After leaving via the nearby creek, Blake did not see him again. Johnson was not heard of until December when some Indians trapping in the Rat River district reported to Constable Millen at Arctic Red River that a strange white man had been interfering with their trap lines. They said the man lived alone in a cabin about 15 miles (24 km) up the Rat and believed his name was Albert Johnson.

At 7 a.m. Boxing Day, Constable Alfred W. King and Special Constable Joseph Bernard left Arctic Red River by dog team in bitterly cold weather to investigate the complaint and to see if Johnson had a license to trap. The previous summer in Fort McPherson Constable Millen had told Johnson he would have to get a trapper's license either at Arctic Red River or Aklavik if he intended working the area, but there was no record of his having done so.

Constables King and Bernard reached Johnson's cabin on December 28. As King later noted in a report to his Officer Commanding:

"I spent nearly an hour at the cabin, knocking on the door and calling to Johnson and informed him who I was and that I wished to speak to him, but he refused to open the door or answer. I saw him peeping at me through a small window near the door, which he immediately covered when he saw me looking at him."

In view of Johnson's attitude, King decided to mush on to Aklavik and obtain a search warrant. This was issued by Inspector Eames. And in view of Johnson's peculiar attitude the O.C. strengthened the patrol by adding Constable Robert McDowell and Special Constable Lazarus Sittichiulis. The four men arrived at Johnson's cabin at 10.30 a.m., December 31.

The location of Johnson's cabin was only a few miles above the junction of the Rat River and Driftwood Creek — a place which a third of a century earlier had been dolefully tagged Destruction City. It was here in the bitter winter of 1898 that four men had died of scurvy while waiting for a break in the weather before continuing their trek to the Klondike in search of a fortune. The Rat River at this junction is marked by a series of rapids so severe that at Gold Rush time the banks were lined with the wreckage of equipment — hence the name Destruction City.

Constable King walked up to the door of Johnson's cabin, knocked, and asked, "Are you there, Mr. Johnson?" He had hardly uttered the words when a shot rang out and King slumped to the ground. Struggling to his feet he staggered toward some brush nearby, while Constable McDowell poured rifle shots through the wall of the cabin to try and draw the fire away from his wounded comrade. But the shooting continued from inside the shack and two bullets narrowly missed the other policeman.

Seeing that King's condition was serious, Constable McDowell abandoned the idea of attacking Johnson's cabin and thought only of rushing the wounded man to medical aid. The two dog teams left Johnson's cabin about 11 a.m. and after travelling all night covered the 80 miles (130 km) to Aklavik in twenty hours. King was placed in the All Saints Mission under the care of Assistant Surgeon J.A. Urquhart.

Inspector Eames now decided to lead a larger party to the lonely cabin on the Rat River. Others making the trip were Constables McDowell and Millen; Specials Sittichiulis and Bernard; trappers Ernest Sutherland, Karl Gardlund and Knud Lang, and forty-two dogs. The Inspector also obtained 20 pounds (9 kg) of dynamite, figuring he might have to blast away the walls of the cabin if Johnson still refused to answer the summons.

The party reached the mouth of the Rat January 5, 1932, and replenished the stock of dog feed at Arthur Black's Store on the Husky River prior to leaving for Johnson's cabin. Travel was slow due to the fact that temperatures since New Year's Day had been hovering around -45°F (-43°C) and the footing through loose snow and willows was extremely hazardous.

A check of the dog feed at the camp showed there was less than a two-night supply left and no chance of securing extra within 80 miles (130 km), so Inspector Eames decided to storm Johnson's cabin the following morning. They arrived half a mile from the shack at noon January 9 — about an hour and a half after day-break at that time of year. Securing the dogs in the timber, they moved forward and partially surrounded the cabin. Approaching from the river bank, the party could hear Johnson moving about so the Inspector called to him to surrender. Johnson ignored the order.

Eames decided they would attempt first to break the cabin door down by smashing it with rifle butts and the three policemen and three trappers fearlessly started to rush the cabin. But Johnson commenced firing as soon as they clambered over the top of the bank. It was then noticed that he had cleverly fashioned loopholes above the bottom logs of the cabin.

Trapper Knud Lang was one of the men who braved Johnson's bullets to lob dynamite at his cabin. Although the cabin was demolished, below, Johnson wasn't even scratched.

Despite the hail of lead, two of the party were successful in bashing in the door as they raced around the cabin, but this only led to Johnson pouring out a steady fire through the opening. When the six returned to the cover of the river bank, Knud Lang told the Inspector he had seen Johnson crouching on the floor of the cabin — which appeared to be about 5 ft. (1.5 m) below ground level — with two automatic pistols.

The party was compelled to build a fire in order to thaw out as the temperature was still -45°F (-43°C). The seige kept up until after 3 the following morning — fifteen hours in all — as it seemed Johnson had an unending supply of ammunition. About 9 p.m. small charges of dynamite were thrown at the walls of the shack but as far as could be seen, they had no effect and most did not even explode. One of the group succeeded in rushing through Johnson's fire to throw a larger charge on the roof, but all it did was to blow a small hole in the roof and not stun Johnson as had been hoped.

The last of the dynamite — 4 pounds — was lobbed against the front of the cabin at 3 a.m. January 10 where it exploded successfully. Karl Gardlund and Inspector Eames ran forward with a spotlight intending to blind Johnson, but he heard them coming and commenced firing. Gardlund switched on the lamp anyway, but Johnson's accurate fire blasted the light out of his hand. The police party then retired to catch an hour's sleep before returning to Aklavik through necessity — feed for the dogs. They arrived January 12.

Two days later Constable Millen was sent back to Rat River with orders to camp 2 miles (3 km) from Johnson's shack to see if the fugitive was still in the cabin. Millen took Karl Gardlund along. On January 16 a party consisting of Inspector Eames, ex-Constable John Parson, Quarter-Master Sergeant R.F. Riddell and Staff Sergeant H.F. Hersey of the Royal Canadian Corps of Signals, Noel Verville, Ernest Sutherland, Frank Carmichael and Special Constable Sittichiulis left Aklavik in another attempt to apprehend Albert Johnson.

Upon reaching the mouth of the Rat, Eames was handed a note from an Indian sent by Constable Millen who reported that Johnson had taken his outfit and left the cabin. Inspector Eames then recruited a party of eleven Louchoux Indians camped at the mouth of the Rat to join the posse. The party set up camp on the river 9 miles (14.5 km) above the cabin. A severe windstorm January 15, 16 and 17 had obliterated all tracks, so for the next four days the party fanned out along the whole of the Rat River Canyon to the Bear River, visiting old cabins and Johnson's traplines, but no evidence could be found of his having been there recently.

Inspector Eames now found that it was impossible to keep so large a party supplied with dog feed and provisions, so the Louchoux Indians were dismissed. The supplies on hand were enough to keep four men going for nine days, so Constable Millen, Army Sergeant Riddell, Noel Verville and Karl Gardlund were chosen to remain and travel as far as the Yukon Divide if necessary. Sergeant Riddell was equipped with a portable short-wave transmitter and receiver from which he was able to receive messages from Aklavik and occasionally transmit back — the first time in Canadian history that short-wave radio was used in police work. The Inspector and

Supplies being transferred from the Bellanca to a dog team in sub-zero weather during the pursuit of the Mad Trapper. The plane also saved the life of Staff Sergeant Hersey when he was shot in the final gun battle.

the remainder of the party left for Aklavik, arriving January 23. He planned to keep hauling provisions to the mouth of the Rat and replace the four searchers after their nine-day stint.

Constable Millen's party scouted a portage from near Johnson's cabin to where the Bear River joins the Rat and from there, into the higher hills that had not previously been searched. On January 28, an Indian who had been with the large party the previous week overtook the four men and told Constable Millen that two shots had been heard the previous day from the region around the mouth of the Bear. The party returned and was successful in picking up Johnson's tracks which led to a thick patch of timber 5 miles (8 km) from the mouth of a creek which empties into the Rat a mile north of the Barrier River.

On January 30, the four-man party split up, Constable Millen and Verville electing to rush down the hill into a creek near where Johnson had holed up and Sergeant Riddell and Gardlund taking the opposite direction. Johnson apparently heard Millen and Verville coming and once when Millen went past an opening in the timber, the trapper snapped off a shot at him. All four men fired a volley blindly into the timber where they figured Johnson was hiding and when there was no return fire, they believed he had been hit.

Millen and Riddell entered the patch of timber and a shot rang out at extremely short range. Riddell scrambled back over the bank for cover, but Millen remained and fired two shots into the thicket. Three rang out in answer. When Sergeant Riddell scrambled over the bank farther away, he saw Constable Millen lying in the snow.

Riddell and Gardlund sought the cover of large spruce trees and began pouring fire into Johnson's thicket. Gardlund watched his chance and while Riddell kept firing, he crawled forward and reached the feet of the inert

Millen. He undid the policeman's boot laces and tied them together to form a handle and pulled the body over the bank. An examination showed that Edgar Millen was beyond help. Johnson's bullet had been deadly.

Two days before this, Army Staff Sergeant Hersey and Special Constable Sittichiulis left Aklavik to bolster Constable Millen's party, but en route met Sergeant Riddell who was returning to report the policeman's death. Sittichiulis returned with Riddell, and Hersey continued on to assist Gardlund and Verville who were keeping watch on Johnson's activities. Riddell brought the sad news to Aklavik Sunday afternoon January 31.

Shortly after, Special Constable Hatting, Reverend Thomas Murray and Ernest Sutherland left Aklavik to relieve Gardlund and Verville. Two days later Inspector Eames left for the site with Sergeant Riddell, Special Constable Sittichiulis, ex-Constable Constant Ethier, Peter Strandberg and E. Maring. En route they were further bolstered by Knud Lang, Frank Carmichael and later at Rat River by ex-Constable Arthur N. Blake, August Tardiff and John Greenland.

Near the Rat they were overtaken by a messenger with news that an airplane was leaving Edmonton, Alberta, to lend assistance. The large group reached the spot where Constable Millen had been shot February 5 and discovered that Johnson had taken to the high ground. They were now in the larger foothills which contained numerous creeks, deep ravines and canyons running from the watershed. Between these creeks was frozen tundra covered with hard-packed snow from the ceaseless strong winds.

Fresh tracks made by Johnson were located February 6, 7, and 8 in three different creeks 4 to 6 miles (6.5 to 9.5 km) apart, showing that he had been crossing the tundra from creek to creek and circling 8 to 10 miles (13 to 16 km) over his own tracks.

The well-known bush pilot, Captain W.R. "Wop" May, flew over the area February 7 and, seeing the scouting party on the Barrier River, landed 2 miles (3.2 km) away on the tundra. Constable William S. Carter from Edmonton bolstered the searchers and Captain May returned to Aklavik to start ferrying in provisions and dog feed. Prior to landing, he scouted the area ahead of the party and saw where tracks — undoubtedly Johnson's — ended at the Barrier River, apparently his campsite. The flight by May was another record since it was the first time in Canadian police history that an airplane had been used to help track a fugitive. Wop May was to prove invaluable — and also save the life of a third posse member gunned down by Johnson.

Another patrol joined the party February 8 headed by Constable Sidney W. May from Old Crow Detachment in the Yukon, Special Constable John Moses, two trappers and two Indians. Next day a patrol led by Constable May went as far as the last timber on the Barrier River and found a recent track made by Johnson heading for the Yukon Divide. Earlier, Indians in the party had told Inspector Eames that it was not possible for anyone to cross the divide alone. To the astonishment of all involved in the pursuit, Johnson, in an incredible achievement, did cross the 5,000-ft. (1,524-m) Ogilvie Mountains which separate the Yukon and the North-West Territories.

With the exception of Constable May, Moses and Frank Jackson, the posse returned to the Rat River where it was decided supplies could be landed easier. These three stayed at the Barrier River camp and on February 12, Constable May and Indian Peter Alexis rode into the camp on the Rat with a note from a trapper, Harry Anthony, stating that a band of Indians had spotted a strange snowshoe track near La Pierre House. The description of the track was that of Albert Johnson's.

In view of this discovery a change of plans was necessary and Constable May, Specials Moses and Sittichiulis, Staff Sergeant Hersey, Joseph Verville, Constant Ethier, Frank Jackson and Peter Alexis headed on foot for La Pierre House over the mountains in the Yukon.

Inspector Eames, Sergeant Riddell and Karl Gardlund flew with Wop May back to Aklavik to obtain larger snowshoes for the party and on February 13 they flew over the divide to La Pierre House, landing on the Bell River in deep soft snow. A sudden storm prevented further flying that day, but on St. Valentine's Day, Captain May scouted the Bell River for 25 miles (40 km) and found Johnson's track which he followed as far as the mouth of the Eagle River in the Yukon where it was lost in a maze of caribou tracks.

Searchers scoured the Bell and Eagle Rivers February 16, finally camping about 15 miles (24 km) from the mouth of the latter where they were able to follow Johnson's trail quite easily as the snow was softer and there was little wind. He had, however, managed to take advantage of the caribou tracks and had hiked without snowshoes in these for about 10 miles (16 km). As the searchers believed they were narrowing the gap on the fugitive now, they broke camp early February 17. Also, another danger threatened — Johnson was headed toward the cabin of a trapper named Barnstrum. Although no one in the party seemed to know the exact whereabouts of the cabin, it was felt the man should be warned of Johnson's treachery. To further complicate things, it had been planned to have Wop May search for the cabin from the air the previous day, but dense fog prevented him from taking off from La Pierre House.

Before noon the patrol, which consisted of eight men with dog teams and three on foot, was approaching a sharp bend in the river when Staff Sergeant Hersey spotted Johnson coming down river only 250 yards (230 meters) away. Johnson saw the posse at the same instant and quickly laced on his snowshoes. Then he made a dash for the river bank, rifle in hand.

Hersey and Joseph Verville — driving the next team — drew their rifles and started firing at Johnson from the center of the river. They were quickly joined by Karl Gardlund and Frank Jackson. In a short time the whole party began moving upstream, some on the river and others on either bank. All this time, Johnson was firing rapidly at the pursuers, but suddenly his fire ceased and he started to run back up river. Before he stopped shooting, however, his deadly rifle had taken a further toll — Staff Sergeant Hersey had fallen in the snow, shot through the lungs.

Johnson was running back on his own tracks, stopping occasionally to turn and fire, and was actually drawing away from the party. He was making for the opposite river bank which was not steep. Called upon once again to surrender, Johnson ignored the command and kept running for the bank, whereupon the posse fired a concentrated volley at him. In the center of the river Johnson threw himself down and began to dig in, using the heavy pack as a cover. He then resumed firing.

But this time, the effect of numbers began to tell. With men completely surrounding Johnson and a few on higher ground firing down on him, he was no longer shooting back.

"At 12.10 p.m., (February 17) it was found that Johnson was dead, having desperately resisted to the last." Inspector Eames noted later in his report. And so ended the 48-day "Arctic Circle war." It had started out as nothing more than a routine investigation and ended in the deaths of two men and the serious wounding of two others. Had Wop May not been able to fly Staff Sergeant Hersey to hospital within two hours his lung wound would have killed him.

All of Albert Johnson's effects were gathered up and checked. A total of $2,410 in cash was found on his corpse in denominations of $20, $50 and $100, as well as two United States $5 bills and one $10. There were also two small glass jars, one containing five pearls, (later valued at $15) and five pieces of gold dental work valued at $12.56.

Firearms found in his possession included a model 99 Savage .30-.30 rifle, an Ivor Johnson sawed-off 16-gauge shotgun and a .22 Winchester rifle, model 58 with cut-down stock. His supply of ammunition included 39 .30-.30 shells, 84 .22 shells and four 16-gauge shotgun shells. There were other miscellaneous items including packages containing a total of 32 pills.

Significantly enough, there was no trace of any written matter found either on Johnson's body, at his cabin or at any of the caches and camps he had made in the area of the Rat River. The two automatic pistols seen in Johnson's hand January 9 by Knud Lang were not located. An old canoe was at the cabin, and about 300 yards (275 m) away, a carefully concealed cache containing a quantity of provisions.

Johnson's 8- × 12-ft. (2.4- × 3.6-m) cabin was constructed of logs. The base of the low door stood below ground level and the roof was made of heavy poles covered with frozen sod 2 feet (.6 m) thick. The walls were reinforced with extra logs and frozen sod. The floor of the cabin was not

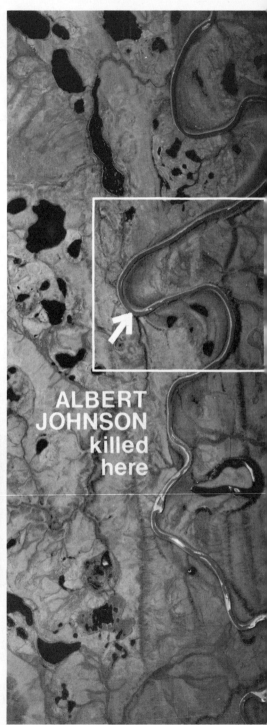

ALBERT
JOHNSON
killed
here

The above aerial photo by Wop May shows Johnson, circle, dead on the ice of the Eagle River. At left is the Eagle River taken from 30,000 feet (9,146 m).

Opposite page, top: Wop May, World War One fighter ace and legendary bush pilot. His skill in flying during the incredibly harsh Arctic weather greatly aided in the search for Johnson.

Opposite page, bottom: Quarter Master Sergeant R. Riddell is generally credited with firing the shot that killed Johnson. He served in the Arctic for thirty-five years and died in 1984 at eighty-one.

as far below ground as it first appeared, but was low enough to provide Johnson with plenty of protection when the seige was taking place.

A physical description of Johnson supplied by Assistant Surgeon Urquhart gave his height as 5 ft. 9 inches (175 cm), estimated weight about 150 pounds (68 kg). He had receding light brown hair, pale blue eyes, snubbed nose, moderately prominent cheek bones and ears set close to the head. The only mark on his body was a small wart, or mole, on his back. Urquhart set his age between thirty-five and forty, and said Johnson's teeth had been well cared for but contained numerous fillings.

The task of identifying the man known as Albert Johnson was one that has never been successfully concluded. All the Force had to go on was that he had told the late Constable Millen in Fort McPherson that his name was Albert Johnson. The Indians complaining about trapline interference said they, too, believed this was his name.

Fingerprints taken from his corpse were sent to Ottawa and Washington, D.C., but they were not linked to anyone with a criminal record in either country.

First reports of the other stranger in the lower Yukon who called himself Arthur Nelson came to the RCMP in August 1933. From the physical descriptions and "lone wolf" attitudes of the two men, it semed likely that they were one and the same, but this relationship has never been conclusively proved.

There are, however, some facts that made it seem likely that Nelson and Johnson were identical. RCMP Sergeant James R. Purdie at Dawson City, Yukon, made inquiries at the banks there to see if he could trace any of the currency found on Johnson's body. The Bank of Montreal traced two bills. One $50 bill was received at the bank as one of a shipment of 100 on September 7, 1926, and the other — also a $50 bill — was one of 100 bills sent to the branch at Mayo on March 22, 1928.

There is no actual record of either Johnson or Nelson having been in Dawson City although Corporal Arthur Thornwaite of Old Crow Detachment in a report dated the same day Johnson was shot said that a local Indian gave a description of a man he worked with on the 12-Mile dredge out of Dawson in 1930. Except for this man having brown hair (Johnson's was light brown) they seemed identical. The Indian said the man called himself Al Johnson and left the district in the fall of 1930 after telling the Indian he was going to the Peel River district to trap alone.

It is reasonable to assume that Nelson received the second $50 bill from Mayo, as on August 30, 1928 — less than six months after the bill was sent to Mayo — Nelson received $680 in cash from the Bank of Montreal there from selling marten skins to the firm of Taylor and Drury.

The firearms found in Johnson's possession were not successfully traced due to company records having been destroyed. But it is significant to note that Arthur Nelson purchased a .30-.30 Savage rifle at the Ross River Post, along with .22 shells, and two of Johnson's guns were a .30-.30 Savage rifle and a Winchester .22. W.W. Douglas who worked for Northern Traders Limited in Fort McPherson recalled selling Johnson a 16-gauge single barrel shotgun and a box of 25 shells on July 12, 1931, three days after he arrived at that Post.

All the persons who had seen or talked to Arthur Nelson between Ross River Post where he was first seen and McQuesten River where he was last seen were eventually shown facial photos taken of Albert Johnson after death. Though most thought it could be the same man, none could be sure. Johnson was in such an emaciated condition at the time of his death that it is explainable that his gaunt features would look somewhat different from the sturdy Nelson.

There was one other question that arose when attempts were made to link Johnson and Nelson. Could a man travel by foot in two months from McQuesten River where Nelson was last seen in May 1931 some 250 miles (400 km) over the Ogilvie Mountains to Fort McPherson where Albert Johnson first appeared on July 9, 1931.

This question was answered by Superintendent Thomas B. Caulkin who commanded the RCMP at Dawson City. He said he knew a man who left Mayo on June 28, 1934, went to Fort McPherson and returned to Mayo in the latter part of August 1934, thus doing double the trip in a two-month period.

Over the years since this bizarre affair, the Force has answered numerous inquiries from persons all over the world claiming to be relatives of "The Mad Trapper From Rat River" as he has been described in numerous articles. In each case the RCMP has patiently checked photos and descriptions, and in each case has had to write back: "We find that ... is not identical with the man known as Albert Johnson."

The only known photo of Arthur Nelson, outlined below, was taken by sternwheel steamer pilot Frank Slim at Ross River Post in 1927 or 1928. In 1931 Nelson disappeared and Albert Johnson appeared at Fort McPherson, NWT, under unusual circumstances. Were they the same person? The mystery remains!

When Guns Blazed at Banff

**Before the trio died from avenging bullets
they had murdered more lawmen than any other
outlaws in Canada's history.**

It was Monday morning, October 7, 1935. A Doukhobor farmer named John Kollenchuk was driving his team along a country road between the communities of Arran and Benito on the Saskatchewan-Manitoba border. It was a sparsely settled region, the dirt road winding past clumps of poplar and around sloughs and pot-holes. Suddenly the horses shied, stopped and refused to move. The puzzled farmer looked around. Nearby was a slough and some bushes but he could see no reason for his horses' strange behaviour. He got off his wagon for a closer look. Then, about 50 feet (15 m) off the road under a clump of willows, he saw two bodies. Once the shock of the initial discovery had passed he realized that the blood-covered objects were in uniforms — police uniforms.

He calmed his horses and headed for Benito on the Manitoba side of the border. To RCMP Assistant Commissioner Thomas Dann he stated that at first he thought the men were drunk, but when he saw all the blood he thought that he was the one who was drunk. He took the policemen to the

At Banff's east gate the trio aroused park staff's suspicions.

The police car in which the killers murdered two lawmen in Manitoba, its headlights shot out at Banff by dying Constable Harrison to protect his fellow officers.

One of the dead bandits, leader Joe Posnikoff.

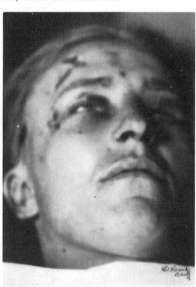

27

scene but Assistant Commissioner Dann had known who the officers were as soon as the farmer reported their bodies.

They were Constable J.G. Shaw from the RCMP post at Swan River and Manitoba Provincial Constable William Wainwright from Benito. The officers had last been seen early Saturday morning leaving Benito in a sedan with three men in the back seat. Next morning when Constable Wainwright had not returned home or Constable Shaw reported to his detachment at Swan River a search was started.

By Sunday the search had uncovered nothing but on Monday morning the police received an anonymous tip from a Benito resident — a youth named Paul Bogarra should be questioned. He was picked up and from him the police were able to piece together a sequence of events, although they would never know if their reconstruction was correct since both officers involved were dead and the three suspects would never be questioned.

It appeared that on Friday Constable Wainwright had stopped a car containing four young men and taken them to his office for questioning about several robberies.

One had been the previous Saturday night when three young men robbed the Smith and Fawcett General Store at Benito. Two of them, their faces covered, confronted W.R. Fawcett with a handgun. When Fawcett resisted he was promptly slugged over the head. Just afterwards his partner, Smith, entered the store. The robbers fled, closely pursued by Smith's son, Oscar. He caught up with them but was pistol-whipped in the face. The robbers escaped in an old model car driven by a third man.

Although Constable Wainwright had received a good description of the car from storekeeper Smith, the latter could not provide a license number. He phoned the nearby Swan River detachment for assistance and officers searched the area early Sunday morning, but found nothing suspicious. The following Friday, October 4, Constable Wainwright spotted four men in a car closely matching the vehicle driven by the robbers. By then a farmhouse also had been robbed by three young men and three of those in the vehicle matched their description.

In Wainwright's office the three admitted that they were responsible for the farmhouse robbery but absolved Bogarra who wasn't with them. Wainwright phoned Constable Shaw at Swan Lake who arrived about half an hour later in a police car. It was a Chevrolet sedan, with Manitoba license plates but unmarked since flashing lights and distinctive color for police vehicles was still in the future.

Since there was no jail at Benito the two officers decided to take the three to Pelly 20 miles (32 km) to the west in Saskatchewan. They left Benito early in the morning, Bogarra ahead in his vehicle. He ran it into a ditch and Constable Shaw made him leave it there and drove him home. When they left the three arrested men were in the back seat but as far as Bogarra remembered they had not been searched or put in handcuffs. He gave their names as Joe Posnikoff who was the leader, Pete Boyken and John Kalmakoff. All were from the Arran district of Saskatchewan about 10 miles (16 km) east of Pelly.

They had obviously murdered the two officers early on Saturday morning on the way to Pelly. Since Shaw had been driving, he was probably

A country road near Benito, typical of the one on which the two officers' bodies were found.

killed first. He had been shot twice in the head, the bullets fired into the back of his skull. Constable Wainwright had only time to turn his head before a bullet pierced his left eye. Shaw had been slashed on the face with a knife and Wainwright stabbed through the neck, also from behind.

By Monday afternoon the police had been able to get a complete description of the three youths from their parents and trace their movements after they had killed the officers. The first specific news of their whereabouts came from a farmer named Sam Peraluk. He reported that three men had invited themselves to breakfast, saying that they were RCMP detectives searching for the killers of two policemen.

Although suspicious, Sam Peraluk did nothing to antagonize the trio. He noted, however, they were all armed with handguns, one wearing a police belt and another a large hunting knife. When they left, he walked with them to their car. They had obviously been drinking and he noticed a jug of homebrew on the floor. There were also stains on the front seat of the car.

After the three left Peraluk's they continued west on Highway 49. That afternoon they stopped at Preeceville, Saskatchewan, 30 miles (50 km) from Pelly for gas. On Saturday evening they attended a country dance — each escorting a woman — at the nearby small community of Ketchen. From there they had disappeared, but were still driving the police car.

By the time the police had fitted the pieces together and sent descriptions of the three to police offices throughout Canada and into the U.S. it was Monday afternoon. Soon afterward the three were located.

During the afternoon, off-duty Detective Constable William E. Harrison of Calgary RCMP was driving along the Calgary-Banff Highway.

Constable G. Harrison, at left on patrol in Banff, and Sergeant T. Wallace died of wounds after the gun battle. Sergeant Wallace's funeral procession was a mile long.

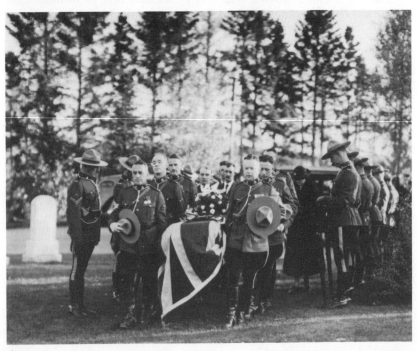

He noticed a Chevrolet with Manitoba plates heading west with three tough-looking men in it, and wrote down the license number. Later in Calgary Harrison read a short news item in the *Calgary Herald* concerning the murder of the two policemen near Arran. Although there was no description of the killers he phoned Sergeant W.E. Buchanan of Calgary Sub-Division headquarters with his information. Buchanan promptly contacted the Banff detachment.

At Banff, the police already knew that something was brewing. Minutes before Sergeant Buchanan's call, they had been phoned by Tom Staples, a gateman at the east entrance to Banff National Park. He had refused entry to three suspicious looking men in a car with Manitoba plates because they would not answer his questions about ownership of the car.

Fifteen minutes later Staples called again and reported the armed robbery of a Calgary couple, Mr. and Mrs. C.T. Scott, a short distance east of the gate. The Scotts were en route to Banff when they spotted a car with Manitoba plates parked on the side of the highway, three men beside it waving flashlights. When Scott stopped one of the men asked if he had any extra gasoline.

Uneasy, Scott told him to help himself if he could get it from his tank. At the same time he surreptitiously stuffed behind the back seat $85 he was carrying. The three began conversing in another language. As Scott and his wife listened, they became increasingly apprehensive — with good reason. They were suddenly confronted with guns and ordered out of the car. One of the men demanded money, and Scott produced $10 he had neglected to hide. Another demanded Mrs. Scott's purse. Then there was a discussion by the three — sometimes in halting English, but mostly a foreign language. There was no doubt in Scott's mind that the trio were discussing whether or not to shoot them to prevent them from contacting the police. Finally, the Scotts were told to get into their car and leave.

Next word of the bandits came from Constable John P. Bonner at the neighboring detachment at Canmore. He reported to Banff that a car with Manitoba plates had stopped at Roy Zeller's service station at Exshaw, a short distance east of Canmore. While her husband was filling the tank, Mrs. Zeller heard a news item on the radio concerning the police killings and the trio of suspects operating a Chevrolet with Manitoba plates.

It was later, when she mentioned the news item to Zeller, that he realized he had put gas in the wanted vehicle. He phoned Constable Bonner who then called the Banff detachment and left for Exshaw, picking up Magistrate R.A. Hawke on the way. By now it was dark.

At Banff, meanwhile, Sergeant Thomas Wallace and Constables George Harrison, Gray Campbell and George Combe were heading east in a police car to stop the three. When Sergeant Wallace left, information that the three were wanted for the murder of two police officers and their description had not yet reached his office. It arrived shortly after the four had left.

As the officers neared the park gate they saw the lights of an oncoming vehicle and blocked the road with their car. It was the Scotts. They were waved ahead as another vehicle pulled up behind them. Wallace and Harrison walked towards it in the full glare of the headlights. Then guns

blazed. The sequence that followed is contained in Constable Gray Campbell's official report. It is understandably terse since it was written when he had gone 48 hours without sleep, felt several bullets pass him and taken two of his mortally wounded fellow officers to hospital, one of them his roommate:

"... just as Mr. Scott's car passed the Police car I heard shots ring out. Sergt. Wallace and Cst. Harrison were directly in front of the wanted car, almost within arms length of the radiator. Cst. Combe was immediately opposite me and we both pulled our revolvers.

"The dust on this part of the road, which is under construction, was very blinding and dense. As the wanted car came nearer to us Sergt. Wallace emerged from the cloud of dust, firing in front of him as he backed up, holding his hand to his chest and demanding more ammunition. I immediately supplied him with same from the pocket in the right car door and picked up a box of ammunition from between the seats. I handed some to Sergt. Wallace and after firing a shot he collapsed. Just as I stooped to pick up Sergt. Wallace a heavy set man pounded through the dust running west. Const. Combe was immediately to my rear and started firing at this running figure who passed on the north side of the car, thus covering my actions in attempting to get Sergt. Wallace in the car. Const. Combe joined me and after getting Sergt. Wallace into the back seat we saw a figure lying under the engine of the Manitoba car with his hands waving. We could not distinguish this object for a few seconds but when we recognized the uniform of the struggling figure we ran over. It was Cst. Harrison who

32

The normally peaceful community of Banff in the 1930s.

Opposite page: Constables Gray Campbell, at far left, and George Combe who survived the shoot-out, and Game Warden Bill Neish who killed two of the bandits.

was lying in a pool of blood, badly injured. I attempted to drag Cst. Harrison to our car though he quickly recovered on assuming an upright position, came to his senses and was able to walk, assisted, the twelve yards or so interval between the two cars in full focus of the headlights of our car. Subsequently it was found that Cst. Harrison had shot both headlights of the Manitoba car as he fell. In the interval from the time that Sergt. Wallace came back for more ammunition until we got Cst. Harrison into the car, there was a fusilade of shots. Cst. Bonner from Canmore and R.S. Hawke, P.M. [Police Magistrate] had arrived from Canmore before we got Cst. Harrison out from under [the] Manitoba car. They immediately took up the exchange of shots.... They then came up to our car, advising me to proceed to Canmore for medical aid, more ammunition and also to advise Calgary and Banff Detachments.

"Sergt. Wallace was in a painful condition, apparently shot through either the chest or abdomen and Cst. Harrison appeared to be losing a great deal of blood from a shot wound in the throat. Just west of Canmore Station on the main highway I passed and stopped a car which turned out to contain Dr. Quigley, dentist of Banff, and Mrs. C.M. Walker who directed me to the nearest doctor. Both men were taken directly to the Canmore Hospital and Dr. Worthington, of Canmore, and his wife, a trained nurse, took charge...."

Constable Campbell returned to the scene of the shootout and learned that Constables Combe and Banner and Magistrate Hawke were still exchanging shots with the wanted men. The officers split up to surround them. As Campbell noted:

"I heard a shot and Const. Combe called 'I've got him' — or words to that effect. Joining Const. Combe we walked towards the body of a man lying on the ground on his right side. Const. Combe rolled him over and took a gun from his right hand. . . ."

The man, later identified as leader Joe Posnikoff, had been hit by three bullets and was dead. The other two eluded capture in the darkness and fled. By dawn a posse which included all available officers and a police tracking dog, Dale, 60 heavily-armed civilian volunteers and Game Wardens Howard Leacock and Bill Neish were taking part in the search.

Towards noon two members of the posse, Dave White and Ed Thompson, drove back to Banff for sandwiches and hot coffee. On their return they saw two men near the road and, thinking they were members of the posse, decided to give them some coffee. As they approached the two disappeared, but since snow was falling heavily their tracks were easily seen. They continued to the park gate where they met Wardens Leacock and Neish.

Just then a government vehicle appeared and driver Archie Keith reported that he had also seen two men. Then a car appeared containing two Banff residents who also reported seeing two men. The Game Wardens commandeered the vehicle and rode on the running boards back to the scene, Leacock carrying a revolver, Neish his rifle. Suddenly Leacock saw a man on his side step into the bushes. "Halt" he shouted.

The answer was two bullets, one of which nearly hit him.

Neish also called out to the man to stop. Another bullet was the answer. Unfortunately for the bandit, he had picked the wrong man for a duel. Neish calmly dropped to one knee and his rifle cracked. The man screamed and pitched forward.

The two Wardens then began a search for the third man. Suddenly Leacock saw himself looking into a rifle barrel and threw himself down. A bullet whistled by where his head had been. This man then threw himself behind a rotten log. Neish, meanwhile, was crawling toward Leacock who pointed to the log with his revolver. Neish took aim. Again his rifle cracked. The man behind the log jerked into sight and lay still.

That afternoon a huge headline across the front page of the *Calgary Herald* noted: "WARDEN SHOOTS 2 GUNMEN".

The official police report, while brief, graphically describes the encounter:

". . . As one of the wanted men ran up an incline, Neish wounded him and he dropped in his tracks in great pain. The other wanted man lay down behind a rotten log and exchanged gunfire with Neish and party. Neish shot the second man right through the rotten log. Neish then expended another bullet on the first man to put him out of his misery."

The official report also carried the sad news that despite the prompt medical attention, the two wounded officers lived only a few hours after the unequal gun battle. Wallace had been shot in the chest and Harrison in the throat, the bullet deflecting off a vertebrae into his lung.

Constables Shaw and Wainwright were buried with full military honors

34

at Swan River and Benito, while Sergeant Wallace and Constable Harrison were buried at Calgary and Banff. During the gun battle, though lying on the ground with his life's blood pouring from his throat, Harrison had taken careful aim and shot out both headlights of the car. He undoubtedly saved the lives of Constables Campbell and Combe since in the headlights they had made perfect targets.

For Sergeant Wallace it was a tragic end to a life of service to his country. He had been a veteran lawman in Alberta, having served ten years with the Alberta Provincial Police before becoming a member of the RCMP in 1932. He also served during World War One with the Gordon Highlanders, winning the prestigious Military Medal for bravery. His funeral procession was a mile long.

Afterwards, there was criticism that he should have been more careful when he challenged the car that followed Scott's. At the inquest, however, Coroner Dr. George R. Johnson noted:

". . . evidence has proven that Sergeant Wallace did not know the full story of the bandits, and used the ordinary methods of stopping a suspected car."

The two officers who survived the initial shoot-out, Constables Combe and Campbell, both joined the RCAF during World War Two.

For Constable Combe the Banff gun battle was his second as a police officer, the first occurring near Drumheller in Alberta where an officer was killed. During his RCAF wartime service he suffered serious injury to both legs and after the war had to have one amputated. He later joined the civil service and worked for various government departments, retiring in 1973.

Constable Gray Campbell became a bomber pilot and won the DFC. After the war he ranched in southern Alberta and wrote a book of his experience, *We Found Peace*. Later he moved to Sidney on Vancouver Island where he founded a successful book publishing firm. On the memorable October 1935 night several bullets whizzed by him — very close by. Over half a century later he still vividly remembered the experience. "A bullet passing through the air creates a vacuum," he explained, "and I can still feel my skin rising on my arm and thighs to fill the void left by the passing slugs."

Marksman William Neish continued in the service of the Parks Department until he retired. He died in 1961 at age sixty-seven and is buried in Banff.

In Canada's history of outlaws and lawmen only one other incident claimed more lives — the pursuit of Almighty Voice in Saskatchewan in 1895. (See *Outlaws and Lawmen of Western Canada - Volume 2*.) In the Almighty Voice fray, however, of the eight shot dead three were lawmen and three were citizens helping the police.

The 1930s trail of blood which began on the Manitoba-Saskatchewan border and resulted in four dead lawmen remains the highest toll of officers to die in one incident while enforcing the law.

Boone Helm —
The Murdering Cannibal

**Probably the West's most vicious criminal, he
earned his reputation by shooting men in the back
and eating at least one of his victims.**

Who was the most vicious criminal ever to brutalize his way through the
pioneer history of the North American West? There are many contenders,
including Billy the Kid, Jesse James, and Henry Plummer whose gang in
Montana murdered over 100 people. But the man generally selected as be-

ing the worst was Boone Helm. He terrorized not only the U.S. Pacific Northwest but also, in the early 1860s, the Crown Colonies of Vancouver Island and British Columbia — better known today as British Columbia.

"Worst of the bad men, wildest of the wild bunch; depraved and bestial was Boone Helm." Not very flattering, but that was how Western historian Hoffman Birney summarized Helm in his book, *Vigilantes*.

In *Vigilante Days and Ways,* another Western historian, Nathaniel P. Langford, wrote of Helm: "He was a hideous monster of depravity, whom neither precept nor example could have saved from a life of crime."

Helm arrived at Victoria in October 1862 but quickly experienced the difference between conditions here and in most mining settlements in the U.S. Pacific Northwest. This difference was law and order. To his astonishment, Helm — who had murdered with knife and gun and had eaten at least one of his victims — found himself in jail a few hours after he set foot ashore. It was, furthermore, the first time he had ever been in jail. And all he had done was steal a few apples, refuse to pay for three drinks

Victoria in the 1860s with the Adelphi Saloon, on the corner at left, as it looked when Boone was an unwelcome customer.

at the Adelphi Saloon, and brag that he was "Boone Helm, and I'm a desperate character."

That his reputation had preceded him was evident from a report of his arrest published in the Victoria paper, the *Colonist*. When Helm appeared before Magistrate Pemberton on October 17, 1862, the paper noted:

"Boone Helm. This man who, it is alleged, bears a horrible reputation in California and other localities on the Pacific coast, was brought before the police magistrate yesterday on remand from Monday last. The prisoner (who is not a bad looking man) was defended by Mr. David B. Ring, by whom it was urged that a prejudice had been created against him in the minds of residents. . . . "

Considering Helm's background, it wasn't surprising that " . . . a prejudice had been created against him in the minds of residents." The citizens probably wondered what had attracted so unsavory a person to the peaceful streets of Victoria. The answer was that the Cariboo gold rush on the mainland was in full flourish and gold by the ton was coming from the creeks some 600 miles (1,000 km) to the northeast. That was incentive enough for Helm. Not that he had any intention of doing honest work; stealing and murdering were his specialities.

Helm was now thirty-four. He had been born in Kentucky and developed into an illiterate, wild and rowdy tough. He could ride as soon as he could walk, was never without a weapon of some kind, and an expert knife thrower. Often he would drive the blade of his knife into the ground from a horse, and returning at a gallop stoop from the saddle and retrieve it. On one occasion when the Sheriff was looking for him he rode his horse into the courtroom to enquire what he was wanted for.

He married in 1848, but abandoned his wife a year later. It was the year his imagination was stirred by news of the California gold rush. He rode over to his friend Littlebury Shoot to ask if he would go with him, but Shoot couldn't because of family commitments. It was the last decision Shoot made. In a rage Helm stabbed him to death with a Bowie knife. It was Helm's first murder, senseless and brutal, the first of many.

Helm escaped, but a reward notice appeared in the *Jefferson City Inquirer* on September 20, 1851. He was described as about " . . . five feet ten to eleven inches high — tolerably heavy built, weight from 165 to 175 pounds — from 22 to 25 years old; determined countenance and appearance, fair complexion, blue eyes. . . . "

He was captured in an Indian camp and returned to Munro County, Missouri, for the murder of his friend. Feigning insanity, he was judged insane and locked up. A few weeks later he escaped and headed west. It was the last Missouri saw of him, citizens little realizing how fortunate they were.

The West saw plenty of him, though. He turned up in California, but not as a miner. There were easier ways of making a living. Sometimes when there was objection to his thieving habits he killed the complainant. Lightning quick on the draw, his killings were always made to look like self defence. Finally he overstepped himself when he shot a miner in the back. As the record has it, "at length he committed actual murder."

California now too hot for him, he made his way north to The Dalles,

Oregon, in 1858, the year gold was discovered on the Fraser River in what would become British Columbia. Gold was also discovered in what is today Utah, Nevada and Idaho and Helm decided to go there.

For protection from hostile Indians, most travellers crossed the Pacific Northwest in groups. Helm and a companion, Elijah Burton, joined a party heading for Camp Floyd, Utah, 60 miles (97 km) southwest of Salt Lake City. They were to go by way of Fort Hall on the Snake River, a trip of over 500 miles (800 km) through rough country and constant danger of Indian attack. Helm's party met with so many obstacles that they returned to The Dalles.

That fall Boone and Burton joined another party leaving the Columbia River for Camp Floyd. They were companions more to Helm's liking — four gamblers. There were two reasons for their trip. New strikes in Montana meant rich miners, and there was the Mormon situation in Utah. The Mormons were disagreeing with the Federal government. So much so that Washington sent General Johnstone to the West with a military force to maintain order. Where there were troops there was a payroll, where there was a payroll there was room for a roulette wheel.

The Helm party packed one with them, along with marked cards, dice and even a race horse! Everything, in fact, to challenge the sporting instincts of red-blooded miners and soldiers.

They left late in October — too late, as it turned out. They were confronted by deep snow and sub-zero cold in the mountain passes. Game was scarce, grub was low and most of the party wanted to turn back. Helm persuaded them to continue, for he knew that a U.S. Marshal was behind him at the coast. In ever-deepening snow the party struggled along. Finally, they reached the Bannock River and the first night in camp one of the gamblers, acting as sentry, was killed by an Indian arrow.

They hastily broke camp at night and stumbled into the harsh cold and a wilderness of snow. Finally they were forced to a standstill, horses played out, food gone. They decided to camp for the rest of the winter and live off the horses. One by one the pack animals were killed and as the weary weeks dragged the five men lived on horsemeat and stray small game. Even the race horse was sacrificed, its meat smoked in chunks. With this food the five decided to make a final attempt to reach Fort Hall ... or perish.

On clumsily fashioned snowshoes, they started breaking trail. Gradually the party strung out, Helm and Burton in the lead. Then Helm proposed to Burton that they abandon the others. Burton weakly agreed. The pair finally reached the Snake River and moved down it to Fort Hall. They were now trying to exist on prickly pear and tobacco plant, the only edible thing they could find. Both were practically starving, and Burton was snow blind.

Finally, Helm decided to strike for Fort Hall alone, but when he reached it the buildings were deserted. Returning to camp, he committed the grisliest crime so far in his depraved career. He shot Burton and cut off portions of his legs for food. Then he started for Salt Lake City. Eight miles (13 km) along the trail he met an Indian who was also starving. The Indian, however, wouldn't touch the human flesh.

Seven months after Helm and his party left The Dalles, the killer — who now was also a cannibal — stumbled into the camp of J.W. Powell, a fur buyer travelling to Salt Lake City. In Powell's party were James Misinger, a French-Canadian called Grande Maison, a Metis and three Indians. The gaunt outlaw explained that his group of six had left The Dalles the previous October, had separated and all but he and Burton had perished. He said that one night while he was collecting wood he heard a shot and found that Burton, unable to withstand the hunger and cold, had committed suicide. Later, the Indian who had travelled with Helm came into Powell's camp. He knew Powell and told the fur trader how he'd met Helm on the trail with a man's leg wrapped in a shirt.

Nevertheless, Powell took pity on Helm, equipping him with a horse, clothing and moccasins. On the trip to Salt Lake, Grande Maison showed Powell a leather bag containing $1,400 in gold dust that Helm had asked him to keep for him. Powell returned the bag to Helm when they reached the Utah town. Undoubtedly, he had stolen it from the luckless Burton.

At Salt Lake City Helm indulged himself with liquor and gambling and when his gold was gone, turned to horse stealing. He joined the Johnson-Harrison gang making forays on the Overland Mail depots. At each post was a corral holding spare horses. It was easy to catch the company men off guard and run off horses to California. Sometimes, in bolder fashion, they raided the corrals of the U.S. Army quartermaster corps.

In 1861 Helm shot two herders guarding an army corral. A few days later, when he was in a saloon in Lodi, Utah, a soldier standing at the bar recognized him as one of the murdering horse thieves. Before the soldier could reach his army weapon, the outlaw had beaten him to the draw and the soldier slumped to the floor, a bullet through his head. Helm cowed the rest of the barroom patrons with his smoking gun as he backed out and disappeared from Lodi and southern Utah.

He next appeared in Los Angeles, a sleepy little town more Spanish than American, with a population of about 5,000. Here he robbed a storekeeper named Horne and disappeared, to reappear briefly in San Francisco, and finally reappear at The Dalles on the Columbia.

Came word now of the Cariboo gold rush in British Columbia, and as they had during the 1858 Fraser River stampede, thousand of miners headed north. How many were murdered by Helm and other outlaws is not known, but many disappeared before they reached B.C. where law and order prevailed.

Others never got a chance to leave for the new gold discovery. Take a gambler called "Dutch Fred" who plied his trade in Florence, a booming mining camp perched some 11,000 ft. (3,352 m) in the mountains of Idaho. In the spring of 1862 the roving Helm appeared and gravitated to leadership of a gang flourishing on the fringe of the camp.

Enmity sprang up between the outlaw and Dutch Fred and one day Helm walked into a saloon where the gambler was playing poker. As Helm stood at the bar behind the gambler he taunted him, hoping that Dutch Fred would draw his six-gun. Helm would then have an excuse to shoot him before he got up.

Dutch Fred, however, put his hands in the air, stood up and leisurely walked over to Helm who had whipped out his gun. Ignoring the weapon in the outlaw's hand, the gambler stood close to the threatening muzzle.

"If you're figuring on shooting," he said quietly, "go ahead. If not ... get out!"

The two men eyed each other. Then Helm's features broke into a crooked sneer. The bartender, watching the pair, felt the tension lift.

"Better let me have your gun, Boone," he suggested. "I'll keep it for you."

Helm obeyed and walked out.

Half an hour later he walked briskly into the saloon and asked for his gun; he was leaving town right away. The bartender handed it to Helm. The cannibal turned and looked toward Dutch Fred who was still playing cards. Helm shot him in the back then slowly left the saloon.

As had happened when Helm senselessly murdered his friend Littlebury Shoot, locals were incensed at the cowardly killing of Dutch Fred. Helm knew that if citizens formed a vigilante group he wouldn't live long. He fled again, this time to British Columbia and the Cariboo goldfields.

Just when Helm arrived is unknown, but the first reference to him being in the Cariboo is 1862 where he and a companion murdered three traders who were carrying some $30,000 in gold. This aspect of his career didn't become generally known until April 4, 1864, when a letter appeared in the *Victoria Colonist*.

While the author of the letter was not identified, he was "A gentleman who knew him [Helm] well" and went on to state: "...he made his way to Cariboo, where he led a life of violence which soon made the country too hot for him, and he, with some associates, killed and robbed three traders, on the trail between Antler Creek and the Forks of the Quesnelle...."

Quesnelle Forks in the 1880s. The bodies of the three men Boone and his companions murdered were carried to the community.

This sketchy information was apparently all that appeared in public print until July 28, 1893. That day a letter was published in the *Toronto Mail* and on August 7 was reprinted in the *Victoria Daily Times*. Its author, A. Browning, appears to have held some sort of government position. He wrote:

"In June, 1862, I was ordered to Cariboo. The year before gold had been discovered there, and from far and near men of all classes and conditions were rushing into the mines. I had camped at Beaver Lake ... and I met shoals of men returning from the mines. Some were dead-broke prospectors, others disappointed gamblers, and not a few who were ready for any dare-devilism that would bring gold to their exchequer. One such I remember well, and the threat he uttered as I gave him good day. The trail leading down the mountain to the Forks of Quesnelle was a mile long.... [Quesnelle Forks, at the junction of the north and south fork of the Quesnel River. It predated Barkerville and was then the largest community in the Interior of B.C. with a population of several thousand.]

"As I came near the base of the mountain I saw on the trail on the other side heading to the little village a procession of men carrying three stretchers. I found on meeting them that they were carrying three dead men. They were found on the trail coming from Cariboo, robbed and murdered, for it was known that each of them was carrying bags of gold dust from Williams' creek to the coast. Who was the murderer, or who were the murderers? Everybody said in whispers it was Boone Helm, a gambler and cutthroat who had escaped the San Francisco Vigilance Committee. He was known to have been on the trail, and he it was I probably met a few hours after the murder was committed.

"There was no magistrate, nor coroner, and the solitary constable was drunk, and if he had been sober was of no use in an emergency like this. A mass meeting was called and I was elected coroner, and after the verdict of wilful murder was returned I was elected magistrate, having a young Jew as magistrate's clerk. The court was formally constituted, and one or two suspicious men arrested, examined, and then let go, for everybody said the murderer was Boone Helm.

"Pursuit down the trail was determined on, and $700 raised to pay the cost of pursuers. Boone, I imagine, got wind of all this, and escaped across the lines,

"When I came back to the coast Mr. James Douglas [Governor of British Columbia] told me our course was as legal as if he himself had signed my commission, and if we had caught and hung Boone Helm on proper evidence it would have been all right."

More information on the Cariboo murders appeared in another letter in the *Victoria Daily Times* eleven days after Browning's. It was written by W.T. Collinson from Mayne Island, one of the Gulf Islands in the Strait of Georgia, where in 1871 he had been among the first settlers. Collinson wrote:

"I see that Mr. A. Browning has given an account in the *Toronto Mail* of the murder of three men in Cariboo in 1862 and noticing some discrepancies I may as well give you a fuller and complete narrative, as I was on the spot at the time. Tommy Harvey, alias Irish Tommy, and myself, left

Antler creek in company with Sokoloski and two Frenchmen for Forks Quesnelle. This was on or about 18th July, 1862. We journeyed together until we arrived at Keithley Creek, where the three aforementioned gentlemen, carrying on a mule and two horses about $32,000 in coarse gold, stopped for dinner, Harvey and I journeying on about three miles to the ferry, where we cooked our repast a la mode Cariboo, when we took the ferry boat, rowed and owned by Jacob Heck, now resident on Mayne Island. After crossing the lower end of the North Fork Lake we made the best of our way for Cap Mitchell's bridge across the North Fork. I well remember this portion of the trail, as I walked it barefoot, my gum boots getting uncomfortable. We paid our fare of 25 cents at the bridge and made the best of our way into Quesnelle Forks, arriving in good time that evening. Now I am quite satisfied that we met Boone Helm and his chum about three miles out from the Forks Quesnelle. We stayed at the Forks next day and saw the murdered men brought in. They had made a brave fight, every man's pistol (good six shooters) was empty, and each man had a bullet through his head. Boone Helm and his chum killed these three men, took and hid the dust, and if no stranger has found it it is there yet, for Boone left the country. I have proof of that, for after leaving the Forks I went to Little lake, seven miles away, to look for some horses to pack in goods from the Forks to Antler Creek, 40 miles, at 20 cents a pound, but not finding any horses, I journeyed on down, stopping at Beaver Lake, Deep Creek and Williams Lake, stopping with Tom Mannifield, harvesting a few days, when I started for Lytton. I met Boone Helm and his chum at Little Bloody Run, just below Cap Venable's, a few miles above Cook & Kimble's ferry, now Spence's Bridge. The first thing I heard was, 'throw up your hands,' and looking up I saw the muzzle of a double-barrelled shot gun about four feet from my head. It took his partner about five minutes to cut my pack straps, after taking my six shooter and purse. The latter contained three Mexican dollars and three British shillings. One of my old shirts contained a good wad of dust, but when the blankets were unrolled the shirt with the others rolled out and a small bag containing bullets attracted their attention and saved my dust, which being tied in the old shirt pocket inside was not seen. They emptied my pistol, gave it back to me and told me to git and not look back. As my road was down hill I lost no time...."

Boone's activities after robbing Collinson are unknown, but by October he had crossed to Victoria on Vancouver Island, then the second largest community on the Pacific Coast. As he clumped along the uneven plank sidewalk with his stiff legged horseman's gait he thought the scene little different from Yuba City, Hangtown or Yreka. Along Wharf Street he noted the same "San Francisco" false fronts on the warehouses and stores, and round the corner on Lower Yates Street the gas-lit saloons seemed well patronized. From some of them came the strains of music and the laughter and squeals of the girls, and there was even the familiar Wells Fargo sign.

But there was a difference. Below the border gunplay was common and in many communities citizens had formed "Vigilante" committees to rid themselves of thieves and murderers. As Helm would learn, they hanged scores of the West's worst desperadoes. But in the Colonies of Vancouver

Island and British Columbia there was official law and order. True, there were under three dozen judges and policemen to uphold the law in an area larger than California, Oregon and Washington. But the few lawmen did maintain order throughout the massive wilderness they had to cover. On October 12 Boone was given a demonstration.

That day he had stolen apples from a stand and visited some saloons but refused to pay. About 10 o'clock that Sunday night he pushed his way into the crowded Adelphi Saloon, Sam Militich, proprietor. Helm loudly called for whiskey. As was the custom, the bartender pushed a bottle and glass in front of him. After his third drink Helm turned to go.

"You forgot something, mister," came the quiet reminder.

Helm turned and surveyed him. "D'ye know who I am? I'm Boone Helm, and I'm a desperate character."

"I don't care who you are," came the barman's calm reply. "You owe me six bits."

Then he half inclined his head to proprietor Militich who was standing near the door. Militich stepped outside and spotted City Police Sergeant George Blake. He beckoned the law over. "A man in here trying to make trouble. Won't pay for his drinks."

"I think I've heard of him already tonight," was Blake's reply, as he went through the swinging doors.

He eyed Helm. "All right, fellow, pay the man what you owe him."

The barroom clamor stilled and Helm suddenly found himself the center of interest. He liked the role, and still refused to pay.

"Then you better come with me," said the Sergeant.

Helm suddenly found himself propelled through the door. Not only through the door but also down the street to Bastion Square prison where he was booked for disorderly conduct.

When minutes later a cell door clanged behind him, it was a new experience. For thirteen years he'd gouged, fought, shot and stabbed his way out of one predicament after another. Gunfighter, horse thief, stage robber, cannibal, wanted for murder in half a dozen places, now he was in jail for a lousy six bits. Worse was to come.

On October 14 the *Victoria Colonist* noted: "Suspicious Character. Boone Helm, represented as a bad character, was taken into custody on Sunday night last, upon a charge of drinking at saloons and leaving without settling his score, and for taking some apples from a stand. Sgt. Blake, who made the arrest, said that he understood the accused had killed a man at Salmon River, and fled to British Columbia. Helen [Helm] was remanded for three days in order to see what account he can then give of himself."

On October 17 Boone appeared before Magistrate Augustus Pemberton, with Sergeant Blake and saloon keeper Militich ready to testify. Suddenly he realized that these people were serious.

He fell back on a plea for pity. He was a stranger, he said, friendless and without money. In fact, he said, if it hadn't been for the warm sanctuary of the prison cell the night before, he might have had to walk the streets.

Magistrate Pemberton was prepared for this ploy and asked David Ring, a local lawyer who happened to be in court, to handle the stranger's

Victoria's Bastion Square Jail where Boone ended up spending a month and, opposite, Judge A. Pemberton who sentenced him. Between 1860-85 nine men were hanged behind the building.

defence. Unknown to lawyer Ring, however, his new client was in for worse trouble than either imagined. In jail, Helm has boasted of his exploits, even relating the fate of Dutch Fred in Florence, Idaho. As a consequence, Sergeant Blake told the court that he believed the prisoner to be a fugitive from Idaho, possibly wanted for murder.

The conscientious Mr. Ring objected to this statement. It was impossible under the circumstances, he told the court, for his client to get an unbiased hearing with this sort of statement being made. Nevertheless, saloon keeper Militich and Sergeant Blake gave their evidence.

Boone was convicted of disorderly conduct and ordered "...to find security to be of good behaviour for the term of six months...." The security he was ordered to find came to $450, the alternative a month in jail. Magistrate Pemberton obviously imposed the stiff penalty to give the Victoria Chief of Police, Horace Smith, time to communicate with Idaho.

Helm, unable to post the bond, was locked up and as part of the chain gang broke rocks for repairing Victoria's streets. In the ensuing weeks, police tried to contact the Sheriff at Florence, Idaho. Either he didn't exist or the letter got lost. As a result, Helm was released at the end of the month. Three days later word came from U.S. authorities to hold him.

What happened from then to May is unclear, but there is a suggestion that Boone went trapping in the B.C. Interior with a man named Angus MacPherson and ran out of food. Only Helm returned to a Hudson's Bay Company trading post.

In his book, *Vigilante Days and Ways*, Nathanial P. Langford quotes from a B.C. newspaper:

45

"Upon being asked what had become of his companion, he replied with the utmost sang froid: 'Why, do you suppose that I'm a ... fool enough to starve to death if I can help it. I ate him up, of course.' "

Langford doesn't identify which paper the account appeared in but it wasn't the *Victoria Colonist*. It has been indexed by the Provincial Archives which has filing cabinets full of cards that list hundreds of thousands of news items. While the B.C. cannibalism incident isn't among them, the Archives also has tens of thousands of copies of other B.C. papers which are not indexed but one of which probably contains the information Langford used.

Another reference to Boone's activities after he was set free from the Victoria chain gang is in the letter already quoted from Collinson. In it he notes:

"The next I saw of Helm was at Sumas in the spring of 1864, I think. He was along with a pack train owned by Dan Harris (alias Dirty Harris). . . . Helm was on his way to get the dust hid at Quesnelle and next day I got on my way to intercept Helm at Yale, but the marshal from Port Townsend was there and took him from Yale to Port Townsend on a charge of murder. . . ."

In his letter Collinson indicated that he wasn't sure about the date of 1864. Actually, it was 1863. On May 1, 1863, the following news item appeared in the *Victoria Colonist*:

". . . a notorious character named Boon Helm, who is said to have committed a murder somewhere on the Salmon River, has been arrested by the British authorities at Fort Yale on the Fraser River, and handed over in due form to the custody of Mr. Brandian, a special officer sent across for the purpose by the U.S. authorities, who has brought the prisoner to Victoria, and lodged him in our jail. The same man was once before arrested by a sergeant in our Police force and held in safe-keeping for some three or four weeks, in the expectation that a charge would be preferred against him by our cousins on the other side, and a request made for his surrender, but, as nothing transpired, he was released and three days afterwards the demand came."

News of Helm's murderous exploits had now spread and when it was circulated in Victoria that he was departing for Olympia there was a crowd at the wharf. It was a send-off to Helm's liking. The local press reported that he swaggered on deck, smoking a cigar, looking anything but penitent as a prisoner. From Olympia he was taken to Florence, Idaho, to stand trial for the murder of Dutch Fred.

Unfortunately for justice, the outlaw had three brothers who came West between 1848 and 1860. Little is known of them except that they all died violent deaths, but the oldest was nicknamed "Old Tex." Tex was prospecting around Boise when he heard of his younger brother's trouble with the law. He went to Florence and bribed the witnesses who saw Dutch Fred shot in the back. As a result, the prosecution's case was weak and Helm walked away a free man.

Then he tried mining with Old Tex, but again came the old urge for travel and excitement. The U.S. Civil War was raging, leading Tex to suggest that if Helm wanted excitement he should head south and join the Confederate Army. Off Helm went, staked by Tex to a horse, some blankets and grub.

A week or so later Helm stayed overnight in Virginia City, Montana, a flourishing mining community which had sprung up around an 1863 gold discovery on nearby Alder Gulch. The rich diggings yielded $30 million in the first three years and attracted some of the toughest outlaws in the Northwest.

Boss of this criminal colony was suave Henry Plummer who had got himself elected Sheriff of the community of Bannock. Plummer applied business-like organization to its criminal operations. His gang of fifty hardened ruffians were styled "The Innocents" and split up to cover various communities.

His lieutenant, Jack Gallagher, controlled Virginia City. Under his direction were George Ives, Steve Marshland, John Wagner, Alec Carter and "Whisky Bill" Graves. All had signed a blood oath against betrayal and on the street they recognized each other by a knot in the handkerchief around their necks. Boone Helm was soon a member of the bloodstained brotherhood.

By 1864 the Innocents had their men everywhere, especially in mine and overland stage offices where they could give word of gold shipments. Some were in gambling houses as dealers, tipping off the gang to the heavy winners. Available records indicate that the Innocents murdered over 100 people from June to December of 1863 alone — over two for every member.

The robberies and killings reached such a peak by 1864 that the miners formed a Vigilante Committee. One day when Henry Plummer overstepped himself, they went into action. As Sheriff he was responsible for the safety of a $14,000 shipment of gold. Plummer saw it safely on the stage, then left to meet with three confederates. Mounted, masked and each wrapped in a blanket to avoid identification, they held up the stage and buried the gold. But they had been sighted by fifteen-year-old Wilbur Saunders. He took word to his aunt, for he recognized the Sheriff by the red lining of his mackinaw coat.

The Vigilantes grabbed the four and hanged them in Bannack where Plummer's gang had got him elected Sheriff. Plummer died wailing his innocence, ironically on a gallows he had had constructed. Then the Vigilantes rounded up other Innocents and hanged them in twos and threes. Before long, of the fifty Innocents about ten had fled and twenty-three had been hanged. Then came a final roundup. Some 500 Vigilantes sealed off Virginia City and five more of Plummer's gang were caught — including Helm.

On the morning of January 14, 1864, as the sun climbed into the cloud-free sky, something more than gold held the attention of Virginia City residents. The street was clogged with people, while every roof top, every window was jammed with spectators. Reports state that upwards of 5,000 were trying to see an uncompleted log building on the main street. The owner hadn't yet installed the roof, and a wooden crossbeam connected the tops of the gable ends.

Suddenly the crowd stirred. "Here they come!" shouted an onlooker.

A lane opened in the crowd and through it came the Vigilantes and their five prisoners. When they reached the roofless building, the prisoners

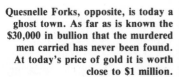

John Xavier Biedler who adjusted the noose around Helm's neck.

Quesnelle Forks, opposite, is today a ghost town. As far as is known the $30,000 in bullion that the murdered men carried has never been found. At today's price of gold it is worth close to $1 million.

48

noticed five noosed ropes hanging from the crossbeam; underneath each rope a three-foot-high wooden box. John Xavier Biedler, whose brother had been murdered by one of the Innocents, stepped forward and adjusted the rope around each man's neck.

"You felt for them, didn't you?" someone remarked to him later.

"I sure did," Xavier replied. "I felt for their ears; the left one!"

The five men behind whose left ear Biedler adjusted the hangman's knot included Jack Gallagher, Plummer's lieutenant. He was over six feet tall, broad-shouldered, wearing an army officer's cavalry greatcoat with a fur collar. His luck at the poker table was phenomenal, although anyone who did win from him was usually found dead the next day.

Another was George "Clubfoot" Lane, horse thief and stage robber. He had difficulty trying to accommodate his misshapen foot to the box's small area.

Next to him was Frank Parrish, dressed like any other miner in a dirty flannel shirt, moleskin pants and high leather boots. Three murders had been laid at his door.

Then there was Hayes Lyons, burly and scar-faced. He had nearly escaped by climbing down the canyon walls near town. Found hiding in a shack 5 miles (8 km) away, he admitted to two killings.

Last of the quintette was Boone Helm, described by one of the vigilantes as "...the most hardened, cool, and deliberate scoundrel of the whole band." When he was arrested he tried using pity on the Vigilantes, the same tactic he had used in the courtroom in Victoria. "I am as innocent as the babe unborn," he told them. "...I am willing to swear it on the Bible."

Among the vigilantes was newspaperman Thomas Dimsdale who later wrote: "Anxious to see if he was so abandoned a villain as to swear this, the book was handed to him, and he, with the utmost solemnity, repeated an oath to that effect, invoking most terrific penalties on his soul, in case he was swearing falsely. He kissed the book most impressively."

The Vigilantes were unimpressed. Gallagher was the first to have his box yanked away. The rope tightened and Gallagher squirmed. Helm watched his quivering body as the rope choked him and remarked: "Kick away old fellow, I'll be in Hell with you in a minute."

Clubfoot George Lane anticipated his end by jumping off his box. One by one the Innocents died.

Finally, as Boone Helm saw his neighbor pitch to his death, he yelled, "Every man for his principles! Hurrah for Jeff Davis! Let her rip!" and leapt off his box.

The *Victoria Colonist* later carried a two-line item headed "Hanged at Last" and reading: "The notorious Boone Helm, who has so long succeeded in escaping the ends of justice, has been lynched...."

For two hours the five corpses slowly revolved at the end of the five ropes strung to the single beam. Then they were buried on Cemetery Hill.

Today, Virginia City has been restored as an original link with Montana's rich mining history. Each summer tens of thousands of tourists wander through the community. The building where the five Innocents kicked their last still stands, and nearby is a row of five tombstones. The inscription on one reads: "Boone Helm hanged Jan. 14, 1864."

The Judge carried a cane instead of a six-gun, wore knee breeches and a cloth cap. Yet with one Constable he fearlessly confronted 1,000 heavily-armed miners. It was the beginning of

Frontier Justice on Stud Horse Creek

A few months after Boone Helm swung from the rafter in Virginia City, another gold rush took place in British Columbia where his arrest in 1863 led to his rendezvous with a hangman's noose. This gold rush was to a region that is today called East Kootenay, some 400 miles (640 km) northwest of Virginia City. Here Helm would have felt comfortable because most of the six-gun packing miners were American, drifting north after the depletion of the California and Montana Creeks. There were saloons, gamblers, and a lawless element that Boone would have approved of, to say nothing of

miners with overflowing gold pokes. But there was also an ingredient that Boone would have found distasteful — law and order — although it had a shaky beginning and contributed an unusual chapter in the history of the Canadian West.

In 1863 gold had been found on a creek called Findlay after its discoverer, but it proved a failure. Then in March 1864 a group of miners discovered a new creek which proved very rich. In the vicinity they had seen a stallion, one of several thousand wild horses that roamed the area, and in its honor named the creek Stud Horse. Since the nearest newspaper to record events was some 500 wilderness miles (800 km) to the west at New Westminster, details of the creek's early history are sketchy. In 1896, however, an article appeared in the *Fort Steele Prospector* with the following background information:

"Bob Dore recorded the first claim, calling it the Dore. Then followed the French, Fisher, Cuddy, and others. As much as $76,000 was taken out of the Dore in one day, the average being about $3,500, producing altogether in three years the sum of $521,700....

"About 800 men wintered in the district in 1864-5. In the spring of 1865 provisions became very scarce.... Many were forced to go out hunting and fishing to enable them to live. It was not until the middle of May that supplies arrived from the Flathead Mission. This was a very prosperous season, and there must have been from 5,000 to 8,000 men in the district. Wild (Stud) Horse creek paid better in 1865 than any creek in California

Judge J.C. Haynes in his later years, and Stud
Horse Creek, a name changed by a modest government
official to the less expressive Wild Horse Creek.

did during its palmy days. Hundreds of men made $3,000 to $5,000 in a few months, and some as high as $20,000.''

To part the miners from their nuggets, a ramshackle community called Fisherville appeared, named after John S. Fisher, one of the original discoverers.

"There were about fifty buildings in the camp, including saloons, gambling houses and others," wrote Dave Griffiths, one of the few miners to spend his life in the area. "Everything had to be packed on horses four hundred miles, from Walla Walla. You can bet we had to pay good prices for what we got. Seventy-five cents was the flat price for everything — coffee, beans, flour — everything. I have seen flour selling in the spring of 1865 for $1.25 a pound; tobacco at $15 and they would soak it in the creek all night so it would weigh more.

"The money taken out in 1864 brought in about five thousand people in 1865, and that was the year that millions were taken out. I knew lots of men that cleaned up from forty to sixty thousand dollars that year. I had two partners that year, and my dividends ran one thousand to fifteen hundred dollars a week, and I would go to town every Saturday night and spend the whole thing. The next year the gold was pretty well cleaned up and the excitement died out, and that was the last of the rush...."

Fisherville was also soon gone, even though it contained government offices, several cafes, stores, saloons and a brewery. It stood on the rich Dore claim and in 1866 was torn down and burned so that the gravel could be worked.

While Fisherville was short-lived, it had a genuine frontier atmosphere generated by colorful men like the "Galloping" Kid, "Overland" Bob Evans, "Black Jack" Smyth, and "Yeast Powder" Bill Benniston. Women were also present, each character consistent with her name — "Wildcat" Jenny, "Axe Handle" Bertha, and "Gunpowder" Sue, among others. Several of the girls combined their talents, which were described by David Scott and Edna H. Hanic in their book, *East Kootenay Saga,* as "many and varied," and opened a "finishing school."

During its brief flare into history, Fisherville was also the scene of a clubbing-knifing-shooting fray that resulted in numerous casualties and almost some unauthorized hangings. No one knows the exact date — one account states August 9 — or the reason why the mini-war erupted in front of Charlie Footier's eating house. There were two factions in the mining camp, those from south of the border and those from elsewhere. The latter were in the minority and largely Canadian-British-Irish. Their leader was a vocal young Irishman called Thomas Walker.

Before peace returned Neil Dougherty had brained Paddy Skie with a four-foot stick of green pinewood that left him unconscious, an unidentified assailant had walloped "Overland" Bob Evans on the head with a hand spike, and a man named Kelly had been knifed in the back. Thomas Walker had shot at Yeast Powder Bill Benniston but, unfortunately for Walker, only hit Benniston's thumb. Walker was then shot in the heart, probably by Yeast Powder who drew a second gun with the hand that still had a thumb.

As with much of Fisherville's history, however, there are several versions of the fracas. One states that Overland Bob fired the fatal shot. But subsequent events are fairly well chronicled. One of those present, D.M. Drumheller, later wrote a book, *"Uncle Dan" Drumheller Tells Thrills of Western Trails,* in which he noted:

"A mob was quickly raised by the friends of Tommy Walker for the purpose of hanging Overland Bob and Yeast Powder Bill. Then a law and order organization numbering about 1,000 miners, of which I was a member, assembled. It was the purpose of our organization to order a miners' court and give all concerned a fair trial. Our organization took care of the ... wounded men and put a strong guard around them. The next morning we appointed a lawyer by the name of A.J. Gregory as trial judge and John McClellan sheriff, with authority to appoint as many deputies as he wished. That was the condition of things when Judge Haines [Haynes], the British Columbia Commissioner, rode into camp."

The arrival of Judge John Carmichael Haynes meant that British justice had arrived since B.C. was then a Crown Colony governed from London, England. The judicial show of force, however, wasn't exactly overwhelming. With Haynes was one Constable, William Young, and they had been twenty days in the saddle getting there from the nearest outpost in the Okanagan. But Haynes was fortunate to have even one policeman for there were fewer than two dozen men to maintain order in a region larger than California, Oregon and Washington combined.

Nor was Haynes' appearance likely to impress the miners in the wilds of Stud Horse Creek. He didn't like the Western style of hat so wore a red cap, instead of a gun he carried a cane, wore knee breeches, polished riding boots and rode a jockey saddle on a bob-tailed horse.

He arrived the day after the street fight, tension still high between the friends of the slain Walker and supporters of Overland Bob and Yeast Powder Bill. But in spite of his red cap and knee breeches, Judge Haynes quickly demonstrated that he was the law. Standing on a stump, the newly-hoisted Union Jack fluttering overhead and the solitary policeman beside him, he told the miners:

"Boys, I am here to keep order and to administer the law. Those who don't want the law and order can 'git', but those who stay with the camp, remember on what side of the line the camp is; for, boys, if there is shooting in Kootenay there will be hanging in Kootenay."

Of the confrontation Dan Drumheller wrote, in obvious amazement:

" 'Fifteen hundred men under arms in the queen's Dominion. A dastardly usurpation of authority, don't cher know,' remarked Judge Haines. But one little English constable with knee breeches, red cap, cane in his hand, riding a jockey saddle and mounted on a bob-tailed horse, quelled that mob in 15 minutes."

He put on trial as soon as possible all of those connected with the gun battle. The proceedings were properly conducted, including a miners' jury under foreman A.M. Gregory. Signed September 7, 1864, the official report of the first inquest ever held in Kootenay declared that Thomas Walker "...came to his death by a pistol shot in a fracas in Charles Footier Restaurant. But by whom the wound causing his death was inflicted, the evidence was insuficient [sic] to prove."

Wild Horse Creek in the early 1880s after the gold rush. All that remains of the community is the cemetery, opposite page, virtually all of its graves marked "unknown." Those buried include the murdered Constable Jack Lawson.

For lack of evidence, Haynes acquitted all involved. Rumor has it that Yeast Powder Bill was given one hour to leave camp but was gone in fifteen minutes. By now, Kelly had recovered from his stab wound and Overland Bob was moving around quite well, though he required three months for complete recovery. Paddy Skie probably never did entirely regain his senses.

Although Haynes could not convict anyone involved in the shoot-out, he did try to ensure that future free-for-alls would be less deadly. He decreed that six-guns could no longer be carried. To miners from the U.S. used to wearing one six-gun and sometimes two, as well as a Bowie knife, this was a startling order. But it had worked at Victoria in 1858 when some 30,000 heavily armed U.S. miners arrived on their way to the Fraser River gold rush, and it worked again.

In October government official A.N. Birch arrived at Wild Horse and reported that he found ". . .the Mining Laws of the Colony in full force; all Customs Duties paid; no pistols to be seen, and everything as quiet and orderly as it could possibly be in the most civilized district of the Colony, much to the surprise and admiration of many who remembered the early days of the neighbouring State of California."

Despite the orderliness which so impressed Birch, there would be two more shootings on Stud Horse Creek, although by then the name had been changed to the less expressive Wild Horse Creek by a prudish government official. Despite Judge Haynes' prediction that ". . . if there is shooting in Kootenay there will be hanging in Kootenay," those involved escaped

54

- NOTICE -
THIS GROUND IS A PORTION OF THE ORIGINAL BURYING GROUND OF PIONEER WILD HORSE CREEK - MINERS - THE GRAVE RAILINGS ARE THE ORIGINALS

DATING FROM 1863 APPROX. PLEASE HELP TO PRESERVE THIS CEMETERY. REHABILITATED BY VOLUNTARY CITIZENS ~ 1953 ~ BE CAREFUL WITH FIRE

UNKNOWN

the noose. The two murderers probably wouldn't have, however, had they faced a jury. As it was, in the manner of Boone Helm one of them met quick justice by a vigilante committee.

The first episode began in July 1867 when a notorious thug, Charles "One Ear" Brown, arrived at Wild Horse Creek with horses he had stolen from a ranch corral. The owners, two Dutchmen, followed Brown's trail until they found his camp, then rode to Wild Horse to report their loss. By now there were three policemen in the community — James Normansell, John Carrington and rookie Jack Lawson. When the ranchers arrived Normansell and Carrington were on patrol but Lawson offered to get their horses back.

Next morning the three rode to Brown's camp. Lawson noticed the wanted man coming down a trail and asked him about the horses. As he did he saw Brown's hand slipping toward the inside of his jacket. Drawing his gun, Lawson gave the outlaw curt instruction to keep his hands in the air, but turned his head for an instant to beckon the Dutchmen forward. It was a split-second error that cost Lawson his life. With a lightning draw Brown put a pistol bullet through the back of Lawson's head. The officer reeled in the saddle and fell to the ground. The two ranchers put spurs to their horses and disappeared.

Brown took the policeman's gun and headed for the U.S. border where he felt he would be safer since he was familiar with British justice. In fact, it was in Victoria's formidable Bastion Street Jail where he had acquired his nickname. His first conviction had been in 1859 for peddling whisky, but a term on the chain gang didn't cure him. In 1861 he was in jail again but refused to join the chain gang and was confined to his cell on bread and water.

One afternoon jailer Charles B. Wright had to move Brown to another cell. When he entered, Brown backed up against the wall with the warning: "You.... If you lay a hand on me, I'll murder you."

In the ensuing struggle, Brown got a headlock on the jailer, but Wright drew his gun and put the muzzle alongside Charlie's ear: "Let go, or I'll blow your head off."

When Brown ignored the warning, Wright pulled the trigger. Charlie lost an ear but gained a nickname, "One Ear." In addition, at the November Assize he came up before Judge Cameron charged with assaulting a peace officer. He got another year.

When Brown was finally released he quickly left Victoria for what he hoped would be a less dangerous place to flaunt the law. Now he was fleeing for he well knew that if caught in British territory he would hang.

When the two Dutchmen arrived back at Wild Horse Creek with news of the murder four miners loaded their rifles and shotguns and quietly disappeared.

In a relentless feat of tracking they found where the fugitive had crossed St. Mary's River on a raft, losing most of his supplies in the rough water. Next they came to Joe Davis' camp where they found the one-eared bandit had got food and continued on a mountain trail. Some 12 miles (19 km) from Davis' camp they met a Chinese. Yes, he'd seen a man with a missing ear; he wanted ammunition but the Chinese didn't have any. On they went, next checking with a blacksmith who said the earless fugitive got food from him. Brown was well armed and boastful, recounting how he had killed a B.C. policeman and how he was going to shoot a couple of Dutchmen at the first opportunity.

It wasn't long after that the avenging quartet crossed the border into the U.S., their horses raising clouds of white alkali dust as they neared Bonner's Ferry. There they met an Indian who had just been accosted by a lone horseman, a one-eared man. He wanted ammunition. The miners were nearing the end of their quest. The *British Columbian* newspaper at New Westminster carried the sequel:

"Leaving their jaded horses at the Ferry, and disguising themselves with moccasins, and etc., they pushed forward until hearing of his having crossed the Kootenay and struck the trail at the head of the lake, they lay in wait for him. Seeing no footprints of either man or beast on the trail, Brown pressed on, thinking himself safe. They soon saw him advancing at a rapid pace, with the remaining pistol in one hand and a knife in the other. Three of them raised their guns, double barreled guns, loaded with buckshot and fired simultaneously, literally riddling his dastardly carcass. Returning on the following day, they dug a hole into which they put the remains of Charles Brown, the thief and cowardly murderer. He lies close by the side of the Walla Walla trail, 43 miles south of the boundary line...."

There was one other killing on Wild Horse Creek and it, too, was settled by the miners, but in less dramatic fashion. It occurred on July 4, 1868, an American holiday that the mining camp celebrated along with Canadian and British ones. By evening the camp was "well liquored up" with miners crowding into Buckly's Saloon for an Independence Day Ball which even featured a few women. About 8 o'clock an Irishman named Robert Devlin began causing a disturbance. Constable John Carrington, however, had been watching events. He came in the front door and Devlin left quickly by the back. But Carrington sensed trouble and advised Chief James Normansell.

Trouble soon came. The resentful Devlin returned to Buckly's about 9 o'clock with his revolver and indiscriminately fired four shots into the crowded saloon. Michael Walsh, a young Irishman, took the first in his shoulder. As he spun round, the second hit him in the back and killed him. The third bullet wounded Cain Mahoney, and the fourth ploughed into the log wall.

Normansell and Carrington heard the shots and ran to the saloon, where they subdued Devlin. The real fight, however, threatened not to be with Devlin but with the angry miners. They quickly made their intentions clear when they looped a rope over a rafter to execute speedy justice. Fortunately for Devlin the two policemen successfully got him to the makeshift jail. But he never came to trial.

The reason dated back to July 12, 1690. On that date the British, under Protestant William III, soundly defeated the Irish under Catholic James II at the Battle of the Boyne. Nearly 200 years later many Irish, including those at Wild Horse Creek, still were humiliated by the defeat.

In spite of the fact that Devlin had killed one Irishman and maimed another, anti-British feeling overcame a desire for law and order. Many of the Irish believed — correctly — that Devlin would be sentenced to hang or given a long jail sentence. As a consequence, one group made plans to free him. They decided that July 12, the 178th anniversary of the Battle of the Boyne, would be an appropriate date.

Some of the men who would willingly have lynched Devlin on July 4 now helped him to escape. They smuggled tools into the jail and on the morning of July 12, after Carrington had brought him breakfast, Devlin ripped a board from the rickety cell wall and pried open the lock. He ran to a grove of trees where a horse was waiting and galloped toward the border. Although Devlin had senselessly killed one man and wounded another, when Normansell and Carrington tried to organize a posse, there was only one volunteer.

It wasn't justice, but for the Irish it was a bit of revenge for a battle they had lost nearly two centuries before. After all, they reasoned, the Wild Horse shooting had involved Irish against Irish. What right did the British have to interfere?

For Normansell and Carrington who had saved Devlin from being lynched but who now had to report his escape, the Irishmen's reasoning was probably puzzling. But as related in the next chapter, some sixty years later another Canadian policeman encountered a similar attitude. The case began as a murder in Alberta and ended amid feuding and moonshine in the mountains of Kentucky-Tennessee.

The Rifle that Hanged Two Killers

The rifle used in the murder was never found. Nevertheless, a brilliant investigation by an RCMP detective led to the jury saying "Guilty."

Detective Corporal Francis K. Russill who travelled some 10,000 miles (16,000 km) on the trail of the killers.

The Alberta community of Vegreville where the murderers faced judge and jury.

Like virtually all citizens, Walter Pursille was law-abiding. He had a quarter section near Manville, Alberta, some 50 miles (80 km) west of the Saskatchewan border. Partly because Pursille's hard-working farm neighbors went to bed early, partly because he was a bachelor, he didn't have many visitors. One fall evening in 1932, however, a car stopped at his gate and his collie dog started barking. Pursille picked up his Savage rifle and opened the door. From the darkness a jet of flame accompanied the crack of a rifle. Pursille crumpled face down and lay still, his Savage rifle beside him. Ironically, although it was unable to protect him in life, it would avenge him in death.

He lay there all night, all next day and the next night. By this time his unwatered and unfed stock were restive. In fact, after insistent squealing the pigs finally broke out of their pen, passing in their helter-skelter flight half a dozen dejected horses standing around an empty water trough.

Only Pursille's dog placed friendship above food, vigorously pawing him every now and again in an attempt to wake him. He howled occasionally

in his loneliness, for now and again he was heard by a neighbor who thought Pursille must be away. But for most of the time, the dog curled up alongside his dead master.

It was early on Friday night, September 30, that the shooting took place but not until around noon on Sunday that the crime was discovered. Vernon Willis, a neighbor's boy taking a short cut home, noticed that Pursille's gate was open, an unusual circumstance. Then he saw the body, beside it the collie, muzzle resting on his master's back.

Vernon ran home and returned with his father. After a brief look at the stiff body, Willis senior detailed his son to tend the stock and left to phone the RCMP at Vermilion. Constable Fred Olsen and the coroner, Dr. Knoll, soon appeared.

"Shot in the chest," Knoll said after his initial examination. "Bullet went clean through his heart — and out the back. Death was instantaneous."

While the doctor was examining the body, Constable Olsen had picked up beside it two distorted pieces of metal that resembled bullets. He dropped them into a clean handkerchief, feeling that they were the core and metal jacket of the slug that had killed the farmer. Then 20 ft. (6 m) away near a shed, he found an empty cartridge case bearing the legend ".303 Savage ... DCC."

As he took measurements he tried to think of a motive for the cold-blooded crime. Revenge? He could not recollect Pursille ever having an enemy. Robbery? Perhaps! He had no money on him. But the house showed no sign of being ransacked, although his .250/3000 Savage rifle had disappeared.

After Olsen made his report, Detective Corporal Francis K. Russill was assigned to the case. Little did Russill realize, as he drove from Edmonton eastward toward Manville, that he had started on a quest that would take him almost 10,000 miles (16,000 km) and several months in Kentucky "feuding" country before he would write "Case Concluded" on his final report. During the investigation Russill would demonstrate amazing tenacity in his far-flung search for evidence.

After a few days of local investigation Russill discovered that robbery could have been the reason for the murder. Pursille had cashed a cheque earlier that week amounting to $571. After painstakingly checking on the murdered man's spending, such as paying off a few threshing hands, the police concluded that the murder victim had about $400 left. The bank teller provided the denominations of the bills paid out, which included twenty-eight $20 bills.

Those whom Pursille paid during the last week of his life were all in agreement on one point — Pursille had peeled the money from a sizable roll. Somewhere, reasoned Corporal Russill, the rash display was noted by greedy eyes, one of which subsequently looked at him over the sights of a rifle.

First on the list of suspects were members of the threshing crew that had recently worked the district. They were found around Vermilion or Vegreville — except for two men, Jack Shea and his nephew, Jim. Shea, in his mid-fifties, was reported to be cruel and boastful, a heavy-drinking man who in his past had trouble with the law in the States — and the scars to prove it. His twenty-year-old nephew was, according to those who had worked with him, clearly under the older man's domination.

The pair had a broken-down Chevrolet but where they had gone no one knew. Their names and descriptions went out next day on a police bulletin.

By now Henry Brace, an Edmonton ballistics expert, had some information about the two pieces of metal that Constable Olsen had found beside Pursille's body. A mushroomed portion, Brace reported, was part of a .303 soft-nosed bullet. The bullet had gone in as one piece, and come out as two. It was a .303 Savage made by Dominion Cartridge. Four grooves on the bullet and the swollen throat of a cartridge case told the experienced Brace that it had been fired by a re-chambered Ross rifle.

The fact that the killer had a Ross rifle, and one that could be identified, was an interesting lead. So far as the missing Savage rifle was concerned, Brace wondered if he could have its "fingerprints" as well, suggesting a further search at the Pursille farm for fired cartridges.

Meanwhile, enquiries continued into the missing Sheas. Reports indicated that after they were paid off they went to Edmonton, then returned to Vermilion where several people saw them a day or two before the murder. After that, they apparently headed for their farm at East End in southern Saskatchewan near the U.S. border.

Ballistics expert Henry Brace, left, identified the "fingerprints" of a Ross rifle on both the murder bullet and the cartridge case, below. The silver and gold inlaid rifle he is holding is one he made himself.

From East End, Constable Ashby reported that the pair sought in Alberta were really father and son, only their name wasn't Shea. They were Kenneth and William McLean. Just after the Alberta murder they had returned to their farm after an absence of months. Near them lived a family called Stauber who were relatives. Soon after the McLeans returned home the two families left in two cars, destination unknown.

While searching the McLean farm, Constable Ashby found some fired .303 cartridges. They were sent to Edmonton for Henry Brace's expert assessment. His microscope revealed that they had been fired from the same rifle that killed Pursille. Then Constable Ashby found a farmer's son who a year before had sold a Ross rifle to the younger McLean. There now seemed little doubt about who had committed the murder. The problem was, where were the McLeans?

Since they had relatives in the southern States, it seemed likely that they had fled across the border. All U.S. Federal, State and County authorities were notified that the RCMP wanted the missing father and son.

Two months later word came from a U.S. Marshal in Tennessee saying that a John Peart and his son, Harry, had been arrested in Chattanooga, trying to sell a car stolen in Chinook, Montana. At the time of their arrest, said the Marshal, the Pearts had been staying with relatives called Sharp at Huntsville, Tennessee.

Three points in the message interested the RCMP: Chinook was just across the border from East End, Saskatchewan; Kenneth McLean's wife had been a Cassie Sharp; and the description of the Pearts matched those of the missing McLeans.

Corporal Russill left immediately for Tennessee. On his arrival he found old man McLean in a Chattanooga jail and son William in Knoxville jail. Russill sent pictures of the pair to Edmonton where they were shown to members of the threshing crew. They were identified as the missing Sheas.

With co-operation from the Knoxville FBI and Deputy U.S. Marshal O'Dell Sexton, Russill now started exploring the back eddies of mountain life in Tennessee. He concentrated on McLean's wife, Cassie, and her kinfolk, the Sharps, with whom the McLeans were staying when father and son were arrested.

Russill's dogged exploration soon uncovered two small stores where the McLeans had changed some $20 Canadian bills. He also learned that he had to be most cautious. His investigation took him to Scott County in the Cumberlands, a country of hill clans where inter-marriage or threat of reprisal closed most mouths, and people were inclined to get somewhat absent-minded where a law officer was concerned.

In fact, as he was to learn, whenever a U.S. government agent had the temerity to venture into the Cumberlands, residents didn't bother sending stealthy messages by grape vine. Someone set off a dynamite blast in the valley and the whole mountain was alerted.

However, with the assistance of Marshal O'Dell, Russill managed to learn that the older McLean was not from Tennessee but Ontario. Here he had married Cassie Sharp. They returned to the Tennessee mountains where son William was born. Always tough and reckless, Kenneth soon fell in with local custom. He shot and killed a man named Harrison in nearby

Morgan County and got ten years in jail. With family help he escaped and went to Saskatchewan where other children were born.

Although his trouble dated back to 1914, such was the tenacity of Tennessee memory that when McLean returned to the state in the winter of 1932, he did not venture into adjoining Morgan County. Eighteen years after the killing the victim's brother was still waiting with a gun.

In defense of the 1914 murder, one of McLean's relatives, Mrs. Lem Phillips, said to the amazed Russill: "... he was a maniac anyway, that Harrison ... low. Why he killed his own brother just a week before...."

Mrs. Phillips omitted to mention that she was suspected of killing her ex-husband, Lem, a few months before. Russill learned, however, that people felt that Josh Sharp, McLean's father-in-law, was the guilty one.

Lem's father, a local preacher, understandably wanted the shooting investigated and raised a fuss. But after Josh "had a talk to him" he wrote a letter to the *Scott County News* saying his son's death "though regrettable was unavoidable," and explained: "The matter had been satisfactorily settled out of court by members of the family and those of Mr. Sharp.

"The situation is of primary importance to our individual families," the letter concluded, "and should be of secondary importance to the public."

In this curiously unreal atmosphere of moonshine and mayhem where old Josh had apparently acted as executioner, then judge and jury to try himself, Russill tried to find the Ross rifle that killed Pursille, or the .250/3000 Savage that disappeared the night of his death.

In order not to arouse alarm, Russill intimated that he was investigating a burglary at Loomis, Saskatchewan, (for which Constable Ashby had the McLeans under suspicion) but when he started asking questions about a Ross rifle, he detected immediate suspicion in the McLean-Sharp ranks. His enquiries were to cause Martha Sharp, William McLean's aunt, to slip her nephew some hacksaw blades so that he could cut his way out of the Knoxville jail. He succeeded, but was quickly recaptured.

When the Warden enquired how he got the saws, William's cell-mate, Gene Ward, a rapist awaiting trial, told him about Martha's sleight of hand. But once Ward started talking, he kept on. What he said was so astounding that the Warden promptly contacted Russill who sped to Knoxville.

Ward, already a two-time loser on morals charges, was a breezy young man with a soft southern accent. Realizing that rape could bring the death penalty, he was obviously trying to benefit himself by co-operating.

He told Russill that when he became McLean's cell mate, the first thing that caught his eye were the words, "William McLean-murderer," scrawled on the cell wall.

"What's that mean?" he asked.

"That's me!" said young McLean boastfully. Later, said Ward, McLean imparted the whole story of the Manville murder, telling how he drove the car and that his father fired the fatal shot.

It was interesting, if true, but Russill knew that men of Ward's character would say anything to save themselves. Besides, he might have read the story in a newspaper.

As Russill turned once again to the search for local clues, the same hunt was continuing in Alberta. Finally, two .250/3000 cartridges were found behind a workbench at Pursille's farm. At first it was thought they would be useful in identifying Pursille's missing Savage rifle, if it ever turned up. But who was to say the cartridges were fired in Pursille's gun? Had anyone ever seen him fire them?

A brother of the murdered man was asked if he had ever been around when Walter Pursille fired the gun. The man thought for a minute. Yes, but it was a long time ago. In fact fifteen years since he and Walter took the rifle out. Crouching behind a stone pile near a boundary fence, they had shot at coyotes attracted by a dead horse.

He guided the police to the site and after searching under the now snowmatted weeds, they found half a dozen weather-stained cartridges. Off to the Edmonton lab they went for Henry Brace's microscopic scrutiny. Despite a decade and a half of summer heat and winter frost, each bore the inerasable marks of the same firing pin, the same faint tool marks impressed from the breech block. Not only did they tally with the shells found behind Pursille's workbench, but now the police could positively identify Pursille's gun if it ever turned up. It was like knowing its serial number.

Meanwhile, 2,000 miles (3,220 km) away in Tennessee, Russill had continued checking the crossroad stores in rural Scott County, still trying to find records of anyone who had bought or ordered shells for a .303 Ross rifle. Soon, however, it was obvious that the search for the Ross rifle was a hopeless one. Not only had none of these cartridges been stocked or ordered, but the make itself was completely unknown.

Undiscouraged, Russill persisted in his search for information on the rifle that the murderer had obviously picked up when he shot Pursille. One afternoon Russill asked the same worn question of James A. Baker, a Huntsville hardware dealer: "Has anyone ever bought any Savage .250/3000 shells?"

Baker recalled that someone had, about a month or so back. But, come to think of it, the man never called back for them. More interesting, the description of the absent-minded customer fitted Kenneth McLean.

"He didn't come back," surmised Russill, "because he landed in jail. Either that or he read in a paper about the arrival of a Canadian policeman and figured it too dangerous to go back for the shells."

From Huntsville it was only a few miles to Oneida, just south of the Kentucky border. Here Russill's persistence resulted in him next day talking to a man called Beattie, operator of a small tourist camp and gas station. Russill's idle conversation led up to guns. When he mentioned a .250/3000 Savage, Beattie said he recently met a man who had one.

He was a middle-aged stranger and had pulled up to the pump with a beat-up car for the not unusual combination of a gallon of moonshine and $2 worth of gas. He didn't have the $2 for the gas or even the $2 for the corn liquor, so he left as security a .250/3000 Savage.

"You-all know the type?" Beattie enquired in his slow drawl. "We-all call it a fish gun, down heah."

"Where is it now?" asked Russill, his interest quickening.

"Well, suh, a man come and picked it up 'bout a week later. Paid the foah dollars and took it away."

Russill produced pictures of the McLeans. Beattie immediately identified Kenneth McLean as the man who had left the gun. By his description the man who later redeemed it was old Josh Sharp, McLean's father-in-law.

The date of the first transaction at the gas pump was just before the McLeans were arrested for trying to dispose of a stolen car. From prison, McLean had probably sent word to Sharp to get hold of the tell-tale gun. By now, thought Russill, it had been destroyed.

Russill's conjecturing stopped abruptly when he realized that Beattie was still talking about the gun ". . . shot away ovah to the right — bout six inches in 200 yards."

"How did you know?" Russill asked.

Because, the resort owner explained, "his old Pappy" happened by a day or two later and, seeing the gun, took it out to try it.

Corporal Russill couldn't believe his good fortune. Because of Brace's recent tests in Edmonton, he knew that any fired cases would identify the gun. He quickly contacted Beattie's "ol' Pappy" and asked to see where he had fired the practice shots. Embedded in the soil were several empty cartridges.

Within hours Russill was on his way to Edmonton with the cartridges. Henry Brace put them under his microscope. The gun that McLean left with the resort owner as security for his gas and moonshine was Pursille's. Regardless of time or place, the science of ballistics tallied the "fingerprints" of the fifteen-year-old shells fired in the Alberta wheatland with those fired in a Tennessee hickory grove.

Back again in Tennessee, Russill's further enquiries about the gun yielded nothing. Probably, as he had surmised, Josh Sharp had seen to its disappearance — forever.

Russill then decided to follow another investigative path. Although the McLeans had been on relief before leaving Saskatchewan, just prior to their arrest in Tennessee they had changed some $20 Canadian bills — and Pursille had twenty-eight such bills just prior to his murder. To see how many the McLeans changed, Russill decided to follow the path of their flight from East End, Saskatchewan, to Tennessee. He discovered that the McLeans used a little known border side-road to avoid U.S. Immigration, then passed through Chinook, Montana. That's where they had stolen the car that got them into trouble in Tennessee.

From Chinook, Russill found their route through Minneapolis where his dogged investigation led to a bank teller who remembered McLean as a man who exchanged $300 in Canadian currency, at 11 per cent discount. He even picked him out of a lineup later on. Since McLean senior had only a cheque for $22.50 for a week's work on a threshing gang when he was last seen around Manville, this sudden affluence was suspicious.

When these and other facts, together with the story of the guns, were presented at a Knoxville extradition hearing, the McLeans were soon on their way back to Canada. It was just ten months after their brutal crime that they faced judge and jury at Vegreville, Alberta.

First to be tried and convicted was William who listened to his sentence of death with pale face. He was no sooner back in his Fort Saskatchewan cell, however, when he made a statement admitting he drove his father to

Detective Corporal Francis K. Russill, at rear on the right, returning to Alberta with the McLeans in the summer of 1933. The two are in the center, the senior McLean who murdered Pursille at right.

the scene of the killing, figuring it was going to be a bloodless holdup. He drove around for a few minutes, heard a shot, then came back to pick up his father at Pursille's gate, noticing now that his father had two rifles. Later that night, as they headed for Red Deer, young McLean said his father suddenly remembered the empty cartridge shucked from the Ross rifle after the killing. It was too late to go back, so Kenneth McLean threw the Ross into a clump of willows, along with the rest of his ammunition.

Although the gun was never found, William's account of events confirmed much of what the police had already deduced.

On account of his statement William McLean appeared as a Crown witness at his father's trial, the old man eyeing him impassively as one incriminating admission after another came from his son. Toward evening on one of the hottest days of mid-July, 1933, a jury found Kenneth McLean guilty. He stood to hear the sentence pronounced.

Asked if he had anything to say, he dryly remarked: "Not much. I'm ready for the rap. I've faced death too often to squeal out of it now."

Perhaps there was something in what he said. Stripped for identification on his arrival, jail guards took note of an unbelievable number of knife and bullet scars. Seventy-seven altogether!

That young William McLean had not given up hope of escape was made evident during a cell search. Two thin saws were discovered in his coat lining. His aunt, Martha Sharp, had originally smuggled four sawblades into his Knoxville cell, and two he had used to make the break that netted him a couple of days' liberty. Now, in Alberta, the other two were discovered, as well as a handcuff key in the knot of his tie. But he had one more escape plan.

During the trial an assortment of McLeans and Sharps had come to Canada. Among them was William's seventeen-year-old brother, Willard. One day, before journeying from Saskatchewan to visit William in the Alberta jail, he bought some revolver shells. An observant Saskatchewan policeman, although he didn't know about the gun, noted the purchase of ammunition and sent word ahead. Willard was deprived of his "do it yourself" escape kit at the prison gate.

The McLeans twice appealed their death sentences but both were rejected. Finally, at the unusual hour of half past three on the morning of November 24, 1933, thirteen months after their crime, father and son walked to the gallows.

Although the investigation had cost some $50,000 in a depression era, those involved, particularly Corporal Russill and ballistics expert Henry Brace, could feel satisfied with the outcome. For Russill there was a final example of the difference in law enforcement in Canada and in Kentucky.

During the trial one of the witnesses was James R. Baker, the Huntsville hardware owner who told Russill about the man who ordered the .250/3000 cartridges but never picked them up. While Baker was in Alberta he and his wife were befriended by Henry Brace. When Baker returned home he sent Brace a letter thanking him for his hospitality. In it was the following home town news:

"...we have had some aftermath to that jail delivery in which two prisoners were taken from the jail here by a small mob and killed. Sheriff Winningham of Clinton County, Kentucky, was killed in a gunfight last Saturday night and his deputies then killed the man who got him. That makes ten men who have been killed near here in the past three months due directly to the killings that these two prisoners did, that started it all. Six have been officers and four other people and frankly I think there will be more of it soon and maybe right here in our own little town...."

Inspector A.L. Duffus of the Royal North-West Mounted Police. He decided that the five members of the Manchur family had been murdered by a sixth who committed suicide.

Mike Syroshka. Did he murder six people and escape the hangman's noose?

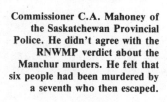

Commissioner C.A. Mahoney of the Saskatchewan Provincial Police. He didn't agree with the RNWMP verdict about the Manchur murders. He felt that six people had been murdered by a seventh who then escaped.

Saskatchewan's Midnight Massacre

"This can undoubtedly be classed as one of the most diabolical crimes in the annals of the province."
Official report, Royal North-West Mounted Police.

The community of Wakaw is some 55 miles (90 km) northeast of Saskatoon in the south-central part of Saskatchewan. In the early years of this century it was noted for two events. One was that a young lawyer called John George Diefenbaker began practising law here before going on to become the Prime Minister of Canada. The other was that in 1916 it was the scene of a massacre that could still be unsolved. Two different police forces investigated, arriving at two different conclusions about the identity of the murderer.

Details of the tragedy are in the Royal North-West Mounted Police's 1916 official report. Although these annual reports are to provide a record of police activities — fact, not emotion — the horror of the crime emerges stark and clear. Superintendent W.H. Rutledge wrote:

"At 11:30 a.m., on April 6, I received the following telegram from Constable Dey in charge of the Wakaw detachment: 'Six people reported dead near here. Murder suspected. If possible send help.'

"Inspector Duffus and Detective Staff Sergt. Prime were at once despatched to Wakaw to investigate. Constable Dey was already on the scene, and Corporal Fowell and Constable Williams were also brought in from other points to assist.

"On arriving at the scene of the crime, it was found that the house of Prokop Manchur, a farmer of the Wakaw district, had been burned to the ground, also a large stable containing horses and cattle had been destroyed by fire, cremating the animals contained therein.

"Amongst the ruins of the kitchen were found the charred remains of Prokop Manchur, aged 46, and his daughters, Antone and Paulina, aged 15 and 20 years, respectively. In the cellar, which was under an adjoining room, were found the remains of Mary Manchur, (wife of Prokop) and her baby, aged 2 years. They were both dead, but the bodies were not burned. Entrance to the cellar was gained by means of a ladder from the room above. Mary Manchur's legs were caught in the rungs of this ladder, and her forehead was against a large stone on the floor. The front of her head was smashed in and part of the brains were deposited on the ground. Her baby was lying by her side, in a position which suggested that it had fallen out of her arms. Upon examining these two bodies it was found that Mary

Manchur had two bullet wounds in her arm and two bullets were also found lodged in the baby's body.

"On examining the charred remains of the three victims found in the kitchen, evidence of bullet wounds was discovered in each. Lying on the snow a short distance from the house was yet another body, the remains of John Mychaluk, brother-in-law of Prokop Manchur. These remains were begrimed with smoke, but not burned. In the centre of the forehead was a bullet hole which went right through the head.

"As the whole Manchur family had been wiped out very little evidence was forthcoming which would throw any light on the affair, and for a time the solution of this wholesale carnage was difficult.

"Two men named Stefinuk and Syroshka were apprehended on suspicion, pending further investigations, the latter being the husband of Paulina Manchur, one of the victims. These two parties had separated from each other, after a short married life, and Paulina had returned to her father's house. It was alleged that this man Syroshka had threatened to kill the Manchur family if they did not allow Paulina to return to him.

"Most exhaustive investigation showed that both these men had complete alibis, and they were later released from custody. The attention of the investigators was then turned in another direction.

"At the feet of John Mychaluk's remains was discovered a .32 Winchester rifle; eight live cartridges were found in the magazine, and one exploded cartridge was found in the chamber of this gun. No person could be found who could identify the rifle, and no one in the district had ever seen it in Mychaluk's possession.

"A part of the plastered wall of the house had not been burned down and one or two bullets were found lodged in it. The bullets taken from the bodies of the victims were found to compare exactly with the ones taken out of the wall, indicating that apparently one kind of cartridge had been used in connection with all the shooting.

"The debris of the burned house was next sifted in an effort to find the empty cartridge cases which must have been ejected from the weapon which did the shooting each time a fresh cartridge was pumped into the chamber. This was a long and tedious undertaking, as the walls of the house were made partly of mud plaster, and had collapsed, burying everything under them. The search was rewarded, however, by the finding of quite a number of empty cartridge cases. They all proved to be .32 Winchester centre-fire cartridges, the same exactly as were found in the rifle at Mychaluk's feet. Some of the steel jackets on the bullets taken from the victims were intact, and it was found that they fitted the empty cartridge cases exactly. These facts were conclusive proof that this wholesale murder had been committed with .32 Winchester C.F. cartridges, the same as found in the rifle in question.

"While these investigations were being carried out, a thorough autopsy was made of the remains. The bullet hole in Mychaluk's head showed very distinct signs of powder burn and the indications were that the weapon used must have been held very close to his head. This suggested that Mychaluk might have taken his own life.

"A sheepskin-lined coat was saved from the fire, in the pocket of which was found a cartridge box containing three .32 Winchester centre-fire cartridges. The box was one which held fifty shells. This coat was positively identified as Mychaluk's, and the one he was seen to have been wearing the night this tragedy took place.

"Further inquiries revealed the fact that John Mychaluk had purchased this mysterious .32 Winchester rifle himself in Wakaw, together with the box of 50 cartridges, six weeks prior to the murders.

"Apparently he kept the purchase of this rifle very secret, as not one person amongst all his friends could be found who had ever seen it in his possession. The storekeeper, however, positively identified this man as the purchaser, and produced his counter check to corroborate his statement. The evidence to hand now pointed strongly towards Mychaluk being the perpetrator of this awful crime, which he concluded by committing suicide.

"Statements were now forthcoming to the effect that Mychaluk, who lived with the Manchur family, had been having frequent quarrels with Prokop and Mary Manchur over money matters, and alleged questionable relations between Mychaluk and Prokop's daughter, Paulina. There were also statements made by Mychaluk prior to his death, which indicated that there were improper relations existing between Prokop Manchur and his daughter Paulina.

"About two weeks before the murder, Mychaluk told a neighbour that he had had another violent quarrel with the Manchurs, and they wanted to put him out and not pay him a sum of $700 they owed him. He remarked that 'if he ever got the Manchur family into one corner something would happen to them like the world had never seen before.'

"In tracing Mychaluk's movements on the night of the crime, it was found that he went out during the evening and was seen returning towards Manchur's house at about 11:30 p.m. At this time he was wearing the coat in which the box containing the three cartridges were found. At 1:15 a.m. the same night, Manchur's stable and house were observed to be burning. It was a very easy matter for Mychaluk to first set fire to the stable which had only a straw roof, and then proceed to the house and there murder the family. The house was divided into two rooms and there was only one door to the house. By standing at this door, Mychaluk would have full view of anyone in either of the rooms. The investigation showed that Manchur's house probably caught fire from the stable after the shooting had occurred.

"Numerous other details gradually came to light, and a strong chain of circumstantial evidence pointed to Mychaluk as the party responsible for the outrage. The fact that this affair took place in a district which is populated solely by a foreign element, greatly handicapped the investigators, it being necessary to work through interpreters all the time.

"On April 14, an inquest was held into this matter, and some twenty witnesses were examined. After a short deliberation, the coroner's jury rendered the following verdict:

We, the jury, find that Mary Manchur came to her death by falling and striking her head on a stone in the cellar; also that her left arm had been perforated by two bullets; that Olga Manchur came to her death from two bullet wounds; that the charred bodies of Prokop Manchur, Antone Manchur, and Paulina Syroshka showed bullet wounds in the vicinity of the heart, which wounds in each case would have caused death, and that John Mychaluk came to his death from a bullet wound in the head, and we believe that each and every wound mentioned herein, was caused by a .32 calibre Winchester centre-fire rifle, belonging to John Mychaluk, deceased, and from the evidence we have and motive proven, we believe that the said wounds have been inflicted while the said gun was in the hands of John Mychaluk.

"This concludes one of the most horrible crimes that we have had to deal with for some time."

Not everyone, however, agreed with the "concluded" verdict in the official report. Chief among the doubters was Charles Augustus Mahoney. At the time of the murders he had been in Wakaw investigating some illegal liquor sales in his capacity as Head of the Secret Service for the Saskatchewan Attorney General's department. A former detective of considerable experience, he didn't agree with the verdict. There were too many assumptions, too many unanswered questions. For instance, was the bullet that killed Mychaluk fired from the same gun? The bullet had never been located. Why was the barn and house set afire? Was there any connection with the fact that the granaries of Steve Makahon were lit by an arsonist at about the same time?

Mahoney had his own theory — someone had set a fire in the Manchur barn (possibly out of spite) and John Mychaluk had gone out to investigate. He had been surprised by the arsonist and shot. The fire-bug killer had then taken his victim's gun and murdered the Manchurs. Also, Mahoney leaned to the theory that the house had been deliberately set on fire in order to conceal the true cause of death, rather than having accidently caught from the blazing barn.

But as a Saskatchewan government employee he had no authority to do anything about his theory. Unknown to Mahoney, however, a dramatic development was to totally change his status.

The Royal North-West Mounted Police had for some time been experiencing increasing difficulty in meeting their commitments to police Alberta and Saskatchewan. Many men had failed to re-enlist at the end of their engagements and transferred to one of the armed services to fight overseas. With most of the able-bodied men in the war effort, it was almost impossible to obtain replacements. In addition, many new duties had been thrust upon the force. They included registration and surveillance of enemy nationals, a constant patrol of the U.S. border (the Americans were not at war with Germany at that time), and counter-espionage.

Consequently, in early December 1916 arrangements were made for the RNWMP to withdraw from the routine policing of Saskatchewan and for the province to provide its own law enforcement. The transfer date was January 1917.

On December 6, Charles A. Mahoney was called to the office of the Attorney General and instructed to organize a provincial police force. He had twenty-five days to accomplish this task!

The problems Mahoney faced were awesome. Saskatchewan was then the most heavily-populated of the prairie provinces and he had three weeks to start policing it — with no men, no detachment offices, no transportation — not even a jail. Despite the almost hopeless assignment, he swung into action. Although the Manchur case was now thrust into the background, Mahoney did not intend to forget it.

By raiding police offices across Canada he assembled senior officers. Constables, however, were a different matter since most of the able-bodied men were overseas. Some of the men he had to accept barely understood the words of their oath of allegiance, while others would have been stumped to spell them. They were spotted around the province as quickly as possible, without uniforms or equipment. Such supervision as they did receive came from visits of the Patrol Sergeants attached to each division — the Inspectors were too occupied with paper work and recruiting to undertake training the men on the job.

There were those in the province, including Regina's Police Chief Bruton, who fully expected the fledgling force to collapse under the weight of its own inefficiencies. As author Fred Osipoff noted: ''The force that took the field on January 1st, 1917, could hardly be called anything more than a group of vigilantes or civilian police. Manpower was strained. . . . It was forty men who set about to police the most populated western province on that New Years Day.''

Mahoney, however, was not only to succeed but to weld together a force that in its short history forged a proud record. Because of the scarcity of trained personnel, he created a flying-squad of detectives and stationed them in Regina under Inspector P.J. Collison. The objective was to dispatch one or more of them to trouble spots as the need arose to supplement and support untrained men in the field.

To Mahoney, one of the ''trouble spots'' was the unsolved mass murder of the Manchur family. One day early in 1917 he called Detective Sergeant George Harreck into his office and handed him the jury verdict. ''I want you to re-open this case,'' he said. ''I am convinced that the real murderer is still walking free amongst us.''

To help him the detective selected Constable William J. Sulaty, a twenty-eight-year-old Russian Pole who spoke fluent Polish and Russian. This linguistic ability was a vital asset since residents of the Wakaw area were largely Russian or Polish, and in his report RNWMP Superintendent W.H. Rutledge had noted that their investigation was ''greatly handicapped'' because they had had to use an interpreter. In addition to speaking three languages, Sulaty had served on both the Winnipeg and Regina police departments and possessed a natural ability to disarm witnesses with his boyish, outgoing manner.

The pair thoroughly reviewed every piece of evidence again and again. Discreet, but persistent and detailed re-questioning of every witness was carried out. This questioning led to new witnesses and new and stranger contradictions in the web of evidence and alibis.

The patient investigation continued through the following year, but with it a growing dilemma. Convinced now that John Mychaluk was the victim of a wild killer, rather than the assassin of an entire family, Harreck and Sulaty were faced with a strange situation. They could prove that their suspect set fire to the Manchur house, but not that he murdered!

Then came a development which again temporarily overshadowed the

Manchur case. It involved three murders, the first major test of Mahoney's new police force.

At Prince Albert on November 15, 1918, Deputy Sheriff James McKay left for Dr. Joseph Gervais' farm to serve a writ for $50. Gervais had bought a team of horses from a neighbor and refused to pay. Three days passed without the Deputy Sheriff showing up for work. Sheriff Seath became concerned and conducted a preliminary investigation. By nightfall the concern became alarm. He reported the disappearance to Inspector Cornelius Sullivan who detailed Sergeant Stanley Kistruck to continue the investigation.

The Gervais farm was at Steep Creek, some 30 miles (48 km) east of Prince Albert, and Sergeant Kistruck had little difficulty tracing the Ford car driven by McKay that distance. However, no one had seen the car return. Probing at the Gervais farm brought answers which aroused his suspicions. He returned convinced that the Deputy had met with foul play.

The following morning, armed with a search warrant, Sergeant Kistruck returned to the farm, accompanied by a posse of provincial police and soldiers. A thorough search of the farm buildings yielded nothing, but as several of the posse approached a dugout on the bank of the North Saskatchewan River a volley of shots greeted them. Corporal Charles Horsley, a soldier, crumpled and slid down the steep embankment.

The dugout was located about 20 feet (6 m) down the bank, making approach hazardous. In consideration for the safety of his small band, Kistruck did not attempt an assault. Risking their lives, two of the men slid down the bank to where Horsley lay, only to find that he was dead. Carrying him by a round-about route, they regained the farm without being fired upon.

Arrested on his farm following the fatal shooting, Dr. Joseph Gervais proved very voluble. He said that on November 15, the day of McKay's visit, he had been visiting a neighbor, Desormeaux. He related that he had seen McKay drive past and, realizing that he was heading for his farm, hastened after him. He feared that two young men who stayed on his farm — draft dodgers — might think the deputy was after them and do him some harm. He had arrived too late, however, for the youths had already killed him, placed his body on a plank and set it adrift on the river. They were engaged in burying the car when he got there.

The two — Victor Carmel and John Baptiste St. Germain — had then taken refuge in the dugout, swearing to kill anyone who tried to take them. It was they who had killed Corporal Horsley. Dr. Gervais went on to state that the two young men had an elaborate system of trenches, passages and dugouts on his farm which he had just learned about, and felt that they would resist stoutly.

Because of the distance involved and poor condition of the roads, it was two days before Inspector Sullivan could lead a stronger posse to the farm. The dugout was rushed, but was empty. Inside was food and water sufficient for three weeks, as well as a whiskey still.

Dynamite was used to seal off the dugout and more exploded in the shore ice of the river in an attempt to find the body of the missing deputy. At the same time, other members of the posse began a farm-to-farm search

Sergeant Kistruck, left, began the investigation of what became the Saskatchewan Provincial Police's first case of triple murder.

between Steep Creek and Prince Albert for it was believed that the men were somewhere in the triangle formed by the two branches of the Saskatchewan River.

Late at night on November 22 a farmer reported to Commissioner Mahoney who had joined the search that two well armed young men had crossed his farm which was about half-way to Steep Creek. While this information concentrated the search nearer to Prince Albert, it was not until Sunday that definite word was received.

Early on Saturday morning, the bandits were sighted on R.T. Goodfellow's farm and several long-range shots fired by police without effect. Later it was learned that this encounter had caused the men to abandon their rifles, bedrolls and provisions. Later that night, cold and hungry, they appeared at the farm of Charles Young, east of Prince Albert. Explaining that they had been hunting, they asked for water. Young inquired if they were also hungry — they were — and shared with them some corn cakes. He then watched them depart towards the nearby Saskatchewan River.

Young, who realized who his hungry guests had been, would have phoned his news to police headquarters at once had it not been for an unusual circumstance. His house, which was to be moved, was already raised above ground. Fearing that they might come back, slip under the house and eavesdrop should he use the telephone, he went to bed.

About 8 o'clock Sunday morning, he phoned the police. Then he went outside. Fresh footprints in overnight snow attracted his attention and he noted that they led to a haystack some 500 feet (152 m) from the house.

By 10 a.m. the yard was full of provincial police, headed by Commissioner Mahoney, and soldiers and civilians from Prince Albert. Because the ground around the stack was open, there was some question about the best method of approach. Charles Mahoney solved the problem by boldly walking towards the haystack.

The Commissioner was no stranger to gunfire. Years before, in a running gun battle with a desperado known as Pegleg Brown, he had received a slug in the chest. The bullet lodged between his lungs and spine and he carried it to his grave.

Accompanied by the local MLA, Charles McDonald, Mahoney circled the stack, noting that tracks did not appear to lead away. He debated ordering his men to fire into the hay, but decided against it. Instead, he shouted for the two men to come out with their hands raised.

There was no reply.

Drawing his revolver, the Commissioner fired four shots into the air. The effect was immediate.

A well-concealed hole half way up the haystack opened and the two wanted men appeared. Though they had thrown away their rifles, they were still armed with revolvers but surrendered them to Mahoney. They were taken immediately to the Prince Albert jail.

Though at first the two youths — one nineteen, the other sixteen — guarded their silence, they gradually became more self-incriminating. Charged with the murders of James McKay and Charles Horsley, they brought up another name — Adolph Lajoie. His body had been found in the ashes of his cabin earlier that year.

Bit by bit Sergeant Kistruck began to piece together a story of lawbreaking that began in August 1917 when Dr. Gervais brought Carmel and St. Germain, who were evading conscription, to the farm. The trio embarked on a crime spree, killing neighbors' cattle, stealing and bootlegging. Successful evasion of the law emboldened them and they began thinking in terms of empire building. Their plan was to acquire more land and bring in other draft-dodgers from all parts of Canada. To this end Dr. Gervais, the master-mind, began negotiating for the nearby property of Adolph Lajoie.

After the agreement for sale was drawn up Dr. Gervais shot him in the head and heart. Then the trio placed his body on the bed and put his clay pipe beside him. Finally, they sprinkled coal-oil around the cabin and lit it.

Because of the isolated location of Lajoie's home, it was almost a week before word was conveyed to police. Constable Garry Tynen investigated and discovered the clay pipe caught in the steel springs of the bed. His report to the coroner suggested that Lajoie might have fallen asleep while smoking on his bed. This theory seemed logical and the coroner did not order an autopsy or inquest.

Emboldened by this success, the doctor then turned his attentions to another neighbor's farm — that of Peter Desormeaux. It was during Gervais' visit to the Desormeaux homestead that Deputy Sheriff James McKay had driven by and later been murdered.

All three were committed to stand trial for the murders of McKay and Horsley. They were found guilty and hanged on October 17, 1919. Under Mahoney, the Saskatchewan Provincial Police had quickly blended into a professional force.

Just over a month after the arrest of Dr. Gervais and his two young companions the Manchur murder case again came to the fore. After consultations with Crown Prosecutor F.W. Holliday, Mahoney decided to arrest Mike Syroshka for arson, hoping that his imprisonment might free the tongues of witnesses even more. Detective Sergeant Harreck and Constable Sulaty arrested Syroshka — the man with the iron-clad alibi — on December 7, 1918.

There was, however, to be another delay. Owing to the deadly flu epidemic which swept the world and took millions of lives in the winter of 1918-19, the trial was put forward to June 17. At that time, defended by brilliant counsel H.A. Ebbels of Saskatoon, he stood to answer the charge of setting fire to the home of Prokop Manchur on the night of the murder. There was also a secondary charge, the burning of some granaries owned by Steve Makahon, a neighbor of the Manchur family.

At the trial, which lasted from June 17 to July 1, there was little doubt in the minds of judge, jury and spectators that Mike Syroshka, husband of the murdered Paulina Manchur, was being tried for murder, though the formal charge was arson. The web of evidence was circumstantial, but at the conclusion of the Crown's case one chain of events was legally clear and a second was morally clear. The first was that Mike Syroshka had gone to Manchur's home on the night of April 5, 1916, and set fire to the house and barn. A few minutes later, attracted by the flames, neighbors had arrived to find John Mychaluk dead in the yard and other bodies visible in the blazing building.

To Charles Mahoney, who attended some of the proceedings, the trial was a complete satisfaction. He had always contended that a seventh person was present that night and had mentally reconstructed the crime on the basis that Mychaluk, seeing the barn on fire, had taken his gun and gone to investigate. He had been surprised by the intruder who had killed him and then taken his rifle and murdered the family.

From the rumors current in the district regarding the improper relationships between the hired man and the suspect's wife, there had been ample motive for slaying Mychaluk — or the father.

On July 1, 1919, Mike Syroshka was found guilty on two charges of arson. In returning the verdict, the jury added the interesting recommendation that on the expiration of his sentence, Syroshka be deported to his native Austria. In assessing a penalty of six years on each count, Justice McKay agreed with verdict and recommendation.

Thus closed the baffling, and perhaps still unsolved, mass murder of the Manchurs.

The Mountie and the Stone-Age Murderers

The Eskimos of the Kent Peninsula had over the years murdered an unknown number of their own people. When Pugnana and his young daughter joined the victims, two Mounties set out on a 1,000-mile (1,600-km) Arctic trek to arrest the killers — with tragic consequences.

Corporal Bill Doak on an Arctic patrol. The photo was taken by author Philip H. Godsell, a Hudson's Bay Company trader. He opened a string of trading posts in the land of the Cogmollocks — a name he gave the Eskimos, opposite, who inhabited the Central Arctic and called their summer hunting region "Kogluktualugmiut".

Crouched over a seal hole on the windswept ice of Kent Peninsula in Canada's Northwest Passage, a Cogmollock Eskimo called Tatamagama kept keen eyes on the ivory marker he had pushed through the breathing hole of natchuk, the seal. The moment the mammal came up for air, the marker would move. But under the flickering Northern Lights of the Arctic night Tatamagama had more than a seal on his mind. His thoughts were swirling around one of the dome-shaped snow houses of his tribesmen a few miles away. There lived Pugnana and his wife, Kupak. Fat, broad of back and capable of carrying heavy packs, she had all the attributes that made a woman desirable.

Tatagama had long wished for a wife but there was a shortage of

women in the tribe. One of the peculiar Oriental customs practised by the Cogmollock Eskimos of Coronation Gulf was that of destroying unwanted female children at birth. No doubt it arose from the fact that life was difficult enough in the Arctic without the hunters having to provide for a surplus population of women. From the Eskimo point of view, they were considered non-producers, not an economic asset to the tribe.

To such an extent was this practice that there was a shortage of young women. Consequently, the rising generation of young hunters were sometimes forced to follow the caveman custom of obtaining their women by force from some other man. Since the approved Cogmollock method of disposing of the superflous husband was a quick stab or a bullet in the back, many blood feuds had ensued. In one such feud alone eighteen Eskimos had been murdered. As a consequence, Inspector Stuart T. Wood, Officer Commanding the Western Arctic Division of the Royal Canadian Mounted Police, decided to act.

Meanwhile, what was worrying Tatamagama was how Kupak's husband, Pugnana, could be disposed of. At last he confided his troubles to his eighteen-year-old nephew, Aligoomiak. They would take Pugnana caribou hunting and one of them would shoot him in the back. Would Aligoomiak agree? If so he'd give him one of those wonderful death-dealing rifles that the traders had brought to the land of the Cogmollocks, and which sold for twenty white fox pelts apiece. With such a tempting prize before him, the sloe-eyed youngster quickly made up his mind.

A few days later Tatamagama and his nephew left the village with Pugnana in search of game. Topping a windswept ridge they ran into a herd of caribou. As Pugnana and Tatamagama discharged their rifles and rushed toward the animals, Aligoomiak fell behind and pulled the trigger of his Winchester. Pugnana pitched forward.

Leaving the body to be devoured by wolves and foxes, they returned to the village and explained how Pugnana had "shot himself." Without resistance Tatamagama moved into Kupak's igloo and took possession of the dead man's belongings and his wife.

There remained one cloud on the Eskimo's horizon: Pugnana's nine-month-old daughter whose cries disturbed his rest at night. Again Aligoomiak was approached. This time he was to receive three boxes of cartridges for his new rifle if he'd rid his uncle's igloo of the child. A rawhide cord in Aligoomiak's hands despatched the child. Tatamagama's sleep was no longer disturbed.

Slowly the moccasin telegraph — the grapevine of the North — carried the story 1,000 miles (1,600 km) westward across the icefields from one cluster of igloos to another. Finally, it reached Inspector Wood on the blizzard-swept chunk of mud and glacial ice called Herschel Island. He decided that the two responsible had to be arrested.

As a consequence, when six months later the sternwheeler *Mackenzie River* chugged into Fort Norman on board was my old trail companion of the Silent Places — Corporal Bill Doak. He was beaming with delight. "Hit it lucky," he grinned, as I led him to my cabin.

"What's doing?" I handed him the bottle of Old Buck rum.

"Just another family rumpus about 1,000 miles (1,600 km) east of

Herschel Island. A couple of Cogmollocks have been murdered by a young Huskie [Eskimo] named Aligoomiak. And,'' he grinned happily, ''yours truly's been assigned the job of arresting the youngster and his uncle and bringing them back to Herschel Island for trial.''

''It's just what I expected, however.'' The Corporal turned suddenly serious as he tossed down a shot of fiery rum. ''Ever since Sinissiak and Uluksuk, the Huskies who murdered those two priests and ate their livers, were given that joy-ride to Calgary; shown the bright lights and picture shows, and given two years at Herschel Island as Mounted Police interpreters, I've expected trouble. Ever since they returned to their people with trunk-loads of white man's clothes, rifles and ammunition they've become 'big shots' amongst the Cogmollocks. Now,'' he growled, ''those Huskies seem to think all they've got to do, if they want a good time at the white man's expense, is to stick a snow-knife into someone's gizzard.''

''They're a tough bunch, those Cogmollocks,'' interjected D'Arcy Arden, the trader from Great Bear Lake who had joined us in the cabin. ''They'd stick a knife in your back as fast as look at you if you get 'em peeved. Take my advice, Bill, and watch your step.''

From Tree River to the Cogmollock camp would be at least two weeks by dog sleigh — with additional weeks waiting for Bathurst Inlet to freeze so that they could leave on their 300-mile (485-km) dog-team journey. They would challenge a land of ice and snow where there wasn't a stick of firewood; where blizzards raged for a week or more; where temperatures dropped to -50°F (-45.6°C) and colder; and where travel would be in darkness except for a brief interval of ghostly half light. In addition, the Cogmollocks might kill them as they had four other whites. Even if the policemen succeeded in arresting the two murderers, they would have to travel with them for weeks — and both had proved to be merciless killers.

Nevertheless, orders were orders. Bidding farewell to Herschel Island's lonely exiles, Doak and Constable Woolams boarded the motor schooner *Fort McPherson*. Through fog and ice and the fury of Arctic blizzards the vessel battled eastward past Banks Island and into ice-filled Dolphin and Union Strait. For days sleep was impossible as the sturdy little craft fought thundering seas and battered her slow way through heavy bottle-green ice. At last she chugged into a rock-girt inlet and dropped anchor before a huddle of small huts — the trading post of Tree River and the one-roomed barracks of the Mounted Police.

Promptly they were surrounded by a fleet of needle-shaped kyaks and walrus-hide oomiaks which disgorged Oriental-faced Cogmollocks upon the deck. All were dressed in their fanciest caribou-skin garments; the women's hair glistening with a fresh — and odoriferous — application of urine.

With a raucous shout Otto Binder, Hudson's Bay factor, and H.C. Clarke, Inspector for the fur company, climbed aboard, followed by Binder's rosy-cheeked Eskimo wife.

Before long a bitter Nor'wester screamed down from the Pole, congealing the salt sea into a white infinity of ice. Soon the sun disappeared for the winter and Arctic darkness enveloped the lonely land. In shaggy swallow-tailed parkas Cogmollock Eskimos drove their ice-shod komatiks, or dog sleds, into the trading post to barter polar bear and white fox skins

Inspector S.T. Wood was
determined to impress on the
Cogmollocks that they couldn't
murder themselves or whites and
escape punishment.

The two Cogmollocks sitting on the
ground below murdered Fathers
Rouviere and Le Roux and
ate their livers.

for rifles, ammunition, knives and copper kettles. From these aboriginal visitors Doak learned that Aligoomiak and Tatamagama were last seen in a Cogmollock village at Kent Peninsula, 300 blizzard-swept miles (485 km) to the eastward.

On the bitter morning of December 3, 1921, the thermometer registering -60°F (-51°C) and stars winking coldly through the Arctic night, Doak and Woolams drove their dog-teams into the unexplored heart of the frozen Northwest Passage, graveyard of the lost Franklin Expedition. With their Eskimo snowhouse-builder and guide, Silas, breaking trail through mountainous drifts of snow and knife-like pressure ridges of upended ice, they crunched over the snowfields. Each night Silas wielded his snowknife deftly, slicing drifted snow into blocks, converting them into a dome-shaped igloo. Here frozen caribou meat and bannock were thawed over the hissing flames of a small primus stove.

After two weeks of bucking biting cold and polar blizzards the dim shoreline of Kent Peninsula loomed through the light of the stars. Then they saw the dome-shaped igloos of a large Cogmollock village, the glow of seal-oil lamps twinkling through sea-ice windows.

Like shaggy bears, fur clad figures emerged from the depths of snow-tunnels. About the two lone Mounties swarmed the Cogmollocks, grasping ivory-barbed harpoons, bows and arrows and scimitar-like snowknives of native copper. A hundred pairs of slanting eyes were levelled with hostile gaze upon the intruding kablunats, or "People with big eyebrows," as they called the white men. The welcome which the usually hospitable Eskimos invariably extended to strangers was lacking. No hands assisted in unharnessing dogs or unlashing sleds. Instead the Cogmollocks stood, hostile and suspicious. From the assembly of figures stepped a wrinkled old figure, an angatkok, or medicine man.

"What do the kablunats desire in Olibuk's village?" croaked the old man.

"Tell him," Doak turned to his interpreter, "we come from the Great White Chief with presents for Olibuk, whose name as a mighty hunter and a righteous man has spread even to the stone igloos of the kablunats."

The mention of presents had its effect. A Cogmollock with a small goatee beneath his lower lip motioned them to a nearby snowhouse, while others unhitched the dogs. On hands and knees they entered the igloo, conscious of the menacing atmosphere. Fur-clad women and children lolled on caribou-skin shingabees, or sleeping bags, spread on a snowbed that covered half the floor space, while two stone blubber lamps cast a ruddy glow about the rancid-smelling interior with its soot-blackened snow walls. As Doak opened his bundle and displayed the presents of knives, needles, fish hooks and scarlet cloth, he was relieved to observe the medicine man lean forward eagerly and hear his grunts of pleasure.

"All this the Great White angatkok sent you, Olibuk," Doak assured him, "because he knows you to be an honest man. He desires your help in bringing justice upon the murderers of Pugnana."

The angatkok remained silent, cupidity battling with his cunning and treachery. Finally he turned to Silas.

"Tell your master that the Great Angatkok of the kablunats must be a wise man to deal thus generously with Olibuk. The men you want are

For Doak, Woolams and other high Arctic travellers
the only shelter was an igloo, built in weather conditions
from sub-zero to a howling snowstorm.

in that igloo at the east end of the village. Agnagvik will take you there and see they go peaceably with you!''

Still fearful of treachery, Doak followed Agnagvik through the village of snowhouses, then crawled behind him into a small isolated igloo, followed by Woolams and Silas.

Aligoomiak, a slim, sloe-eyed youth of eighteen, was devouring a dish of ookchuk, or seal blubber, and except for a fleeting smile, paid scant attention. Tatamagama, by contrast, avoided the Mountie's eyes. Squatting on the snowbed, Doak made known his errand. With Oriental fatalism not the slightest attempt was made by either of the murderers to evade capture. In a few minutes the arrest of Aligoomiak and his uncle, Tatamagama, had been accomplished.

Still, at any moment their fellow-tribesmen might undergo a change of attitude. Quickly hitching up their dogs, they headed west across the icefields. As the dim shoreline of Kent Peninsula was enfolded in the gloom of Arctic darkness, Doak turned to Woolams. "We'll keep going all night," he said. "Those Cogmollocks could just change their minds and try to harpoon us while we're sleeping...."

On through an endless succession of dark Arctic days and nights they drove westward. They were aware that unseen danger might lurk since they were still in the heart of the Cogmollock hunting grounds, with hunting parties scattered about the icefields in search of polar bears and seals.

Then without warning a blizzard broke upon them from the northwest with the fierce impetuosity of the Arctic. Bedding and grub were tossed into a partly-erected night igloo and the remaining baggage lashed tightly to the sled to prevent it being whirled away in the fierce blasts. Frantically Silas wielded his copper snowknife while Doak and Woolams fitted the last snowblocks in place. Safely within the snowhouse they waited for six days as the storm raged with such fury that nobody dared venture out lest they be whipped away to certain death.

As suddenly as it had arisen the gale abated. Then they got a lucky shot at a prowling polar bear, providing badly needed meat for their dogs and themselves. At last the barracks at Tree River loomed through the ghostly half-light. Not only had the prisoners failed to give any trouble, but

Firewood was non- existent, a primus stove
the only way of preparing hot food.
The frost on the officer's mustache indicates the temperature.

Aligoomiak, always quick and cheerful, had helped to hitch and unhitch the sleigh dogs, unload sleds and build the nightly igloo. Doak, always partial to Eskimos, had taken a liking to him.

Since there was no cell in which to confine the prisoners, and to shackle them in the biting cold was cruelty, Doak assigned them routine work. They caught seals for dog feed, mended sleighs, and did odd jobs around the barracks.

It was now the end of March. The sun had emerged from its winter hibernation and began to circle the pale blue sky. Seals emerged from their holes to bask on the melting sea-ice and Woolams departed with Tatamagama and Silas for an Eskimo seal-camp 8 miles (13 km) to the westward. Here they joined Clarke, the Hudson's Bay Inspector, shooting seals to supplement the dog feed. The only two white men left at Tree River were Otto Binder at the Hudson's Bay Post and Corporal Doak.

Out at the Eskimo seal-camp next morning, Clarke and Woolams decided to go further afield in search of seal. As they potted the bullet-headed mammals and grabbed them before they slid back into the sea, Woolams' attention became fixed on a dog-team being driven frantically from the direction of the seal-camp. Time and again a walrus-hide lash rose and fell with a report like a rifle shot, accompanied by the terrified howling of the racing sleigh-dogs. It was Silas.

Jerking his dogs to a halt, he exploded in a torrent of words. "Aligoomiak! He kill Doak. Kill Binder. Come seal-camp with gun." He met the astonished eyes of Woolams. "Kill you, too!"

Pale and speechless, unable to realize the full portent of the Eskimo's message, Constable Woolams learned that shortly after he and Clarke had departed that morning Aligoomiak had arrived at the seal-camp, rifle in hand. He intended to shoot both whites, take the Mounted Police dogs and return to his people. Only the fact that they'd gone further afield had probably saved them from being murdered in cold blood. Taku, the head man at the camp, had secretly despatched his son to warn the whites while his wife was feeding the hungry young Cogmollock.

Woolams leapt for his sled, the snapping lash sending his huskies hurtling over the sea ice. The Constable's mind was in a turmoil. Bill Doak dead! Killed by that little Cogmollock! Hell! Taku's son must have got the story all cockeyed. Sure — that must be it!

As Taku's igloo loomed before him, Woolams sprang from his sled, dived into the snow-tunnel and stumbled. Next moment he found himself gazing into the muzzle of a Winchester. Along the shining barrel Aligoomiak's eye leered in hate. Then the igloo rocked to a thunderous detonation. Orange flame flashed in his eyes. A bullet nicked his ear. Hot anger seered within him as he leapt upon Aligoomiak. Someone thrust a rawhide line into his hand. Twisting it around his flailing wrists he yanked the prisoner through the icy tunnel and lashed him on the sled. Then he set the huskies careening towards the barracks 15 miles (25 km) away, Silas, Clarke and Tatamagama padding swiftly in the rear.

Reaching the trading post, Woolams shouldered through the door. On the fireless stove sat a pot half-filled with frozen porridge. Empty breakfast dishes lay about the table. Over the ice-locked bay hung a brooding silence.

Woolams swung about at the soft pad pad of Silas' mukluks. "Come quick. Me see something on ice."

Following the direction of Silas' outstretched finger, Woolams saw what appeared to be a caribou lying between trading post and barracks. Padding swiftly across the intervening distance they stood beside it.

Outstretched on his face was the body of Otto Binder. He had been shot through the heart. Leaving the dead trader they ran to the Mounted Police shack. Fearfully, Woolams swung open the door.

Save for the biting cold all seemed in order. Then, as his eyes swung to the bunk, he blanched. There lay Bill Doak, his sightless eyes staring straight towards him, his frozen features moulded in a grey mask of agony. Bill Doak, the genial friend of every trapper, trader and riverman from the Arctic to the Rockies, had gone on his last long trail.

A hasty examination showed that the bullet had struck Doak's thighbone and been deflected into his body. Near the stove lay an empty .30-.30 shell. Beneath the broken windowpane, overlooking where Binder had been shot, was another empty shell. Outside, the door of the lean-to storehouse was ajar and one of the .30-.30 rifles and some cartridges were gone.

But so isolated was Tree River that not for nearly five months did news of the tragedy reach Inspector Wood at Herschel Island. It was brought by the sturdy *Fort McPherson*. As the vessel chugged into the cove those calling a welcome quickly sensed something was wrong. Answering shouts carried no enthusiasm. Suddenly a question arose: "Where was Bill Doak?" It wasn't like the boisterous Bill to be backward in shouting a greeting.

As the gangplank clattered on the shingly beach the faces of the crew warned that something was amiss. Swiftly the horrible news spread. Bill Doak was dead — murdered by the Cogmollocks! Grim-faced, Constable Woolams led his prisoners ashore and reported the tragic deaths of Corporal Doak and Otto Binder. Gloom settled over the Polar outpost. Before long the moccasin telegraph carried the word along the 2,000-mile (3,220-km) Mackenzie-Athabasca Valley. Even the Yellowknife and Dog Rib Indians far to the south heard with sorrow and anger the killing of the "Smiling Mountie."

The prisoners were kept in the guardhouse at Herschel Island, permitted out only for daily exercise. But as time passed their freedom was increased until Tatamagama became official seal hunter for the Mounted Police. Aligoomiak, looking like an Oriental houseboy in white ducks and shoes, became choreman for the Inspector's wife.

To the south, meanwhile, arrangements were underway to bring the pair to trial. The problems of administering justice in the Arctic were formidable. The entire judicial party — including the hangman in case he was needed — had to make a round trip of 5,000 miles (8,000 km) to a region without a road, railway, telephone or telegraph, hotel or electricity.

As a consequence, in the summer of 1923, one morning all was bustle at the Dunvegan Railway yard near Edmonton. The "Muskeg Limited" was set to leave for the end of steel at Fort McMurray to connect with the sternwheelers ploughing their 2,000-mile (3,220-km) voyage to the Arctic. Mingling with Indians and trappers was the judicial party, leaving on their journey to carry the white man's law to the Land of the Midnight Sun.

The youthful Aligoomiak, above, murdered four people, two at the instigation of Tatamagama, center of the photo at upper right.

The Tree River Post where Corporal Doak was murdered.

Grouped around grey-haired Judge Dubuc were lawyers for the prosecution and defence, a Mounted Police escort in scarlet and gold and "Mr. Brown," the hangman.

Two days later the judicial party reached the end-of-steel and transferred to the sternwheeler *Athabasca River*. Weeks later they reached that frozen chunk of glacial ice with its counterpane of soil called Herschel Island, where the "Bone house" of the Pacific Whaling Company was converted into a courtroom and the task of empanelling a jury of trappers, traders, sailors and beachcombers commenced. Smiling, Aligoomiak hopped into the dock in his white ducks. Noticing that one of the jurors lacked a seat, he slipped outside, returned with an extra chair, and stepped jauntily back into the dock.

The trial continued day after day: hangman, prisoners, judge and jury mingling during recess upon the beach. Here Aligoomiak was frequently engaged in a friendly game of poker with the hangman, to whom he'd taken quite a fancy.

Questioned about the killing of Doak, Aligoomiak became the soul of frankness. Doak had spoken to him sharply that fatal day, and he was mad. He was convinced that the Mountie intended to kill him, and, Eskimo fashion, was merely waiting a chance to knife or shoot him in the back first. He had that night decided to kill Doak. Near sunrise he'd crept quietly from the Police shack, forced the door of the lean-to, and grabbed a rifle and four cartridges. He'd stood by the stove, taken deliberate aim at Doak's thigh — intending merely to wound and hurt him — and fired.

The Mountie had lived about four hours and had asked him frequently why he had done this thing. When Doak died Aligoomiak decided he might as well kill Binder, too. Standing beside the window he'd waited for the trader to start across the ice on his morning visit. Half way to the barracks Aligoomiak's second bullet had felled him. Then, since he'd found white men could be killed so easily, Aligoomiak decided to kill the two remaining whites and return to his people.

The evidence against Aligoomiak and his uncle was overwhelming. Two Americans, Radford and Street, had been murdered by this tribe only a few years before; then Fathers Rouviere and Le Roux had been slain. Now a Hudson's Bay trader and a Mounted Policeman had succumbed to Cogmollock bullets. If something wasn't done, it would be unsafe for white men to venture into Coronation Gulf.

As the death sentence was passed upon them, Aligoomiak grinned, stepped from the dock and handed a cigarette to Judge Dubuc who'd just decreed his death.

In the ghostly twilight of a February dawn, a group of Eskimos gazed through the half-light at Herschel Island's barracks. With measured step four Mounties crunched towards the "bone-house." Between them, their faces registering mingled apathy and defiance, shuffled Aligoomiak and his uncle. The door slammed ominously.

Then on frosted hinges it creaked open. Four grey-faced Mounties and the hangman tramped back. Pugnana, his daughter, Otto Binder and Constable Bill Doak had been avenged.

Death Duel in the Crowsnest Pass

The train journey was supposed to be routine. Instead it resulted in Canada's last train holdup and the highest toll of dead lawmen in Alberta's history.

Tom Bassoff.

A re-enactment of the cafe duel showing the bodies of the two lawmen. Tom Bassoff deliberately killed Constable Bailey who had tripped in the doorway. He was unhurt during the gun battle inside the building.

It was August 2, 1920, a beautiful day in the Crowsnest Pass which straddles the B.C.-Alberta border. Past Coleman, Conductor Samuel E. Jones of Canadian Pacific Train No. 63 had just finished taking tickets and went back to the baggage car. Suddenly a voice commanded: "Hands up...."

As Conductor Jones glanced around he saw a man with a gun. Instead of obeying he bravely reached up to the emergency cord to stop the train.

"Leave cord alone and sit down," the man ordered, emphasizing his words with a shot at the Conductor. The train kept rolling since a single buzz was not the stop signal. Unknown to the Conductor, however, the signal wasn't working properly. The engineer heard three buzzes which

meant stop the train at the next place, a siding called Sentinel, instead of at Crowsnest.

Two other men appeared and herded train crew and passengers to the rear. Conductor Jones now recognized the three as having boarded the train at Lethbridge with tickets for Crowsnest on the B.C.-Alberta border. As he later recalled: "...I was behind brakeman Hickey, and another man was right behind me and he kept pushing me and I kept pushing Hickey.

"He got us all on the platform and made all the passengers go back but kept brakeman Hickey and myself together.... We came to the station (Sentinel) and the engine stopped. This man said, 'Who stopped the train?'

"I said, 'I cannot say, I didn't stop it....' "

A few miles short of their destination the three then got off, carrying two bundles of blankets and a suitcase. With a parting shot in the direction of Conductor Jones, they casually headed into the nearby woods. Thus by accident began what would become the biggest manhunt in Alberta's history and the most costly in terms of dead lawmen.

The three bandits were later identified as Russians: Alex Auloff, Tom Bassoff and George Akoff. Their motive in robbing the train remains unknown, although local legend centers on "Emperor Pic," the bootleg king of the Crowsnest Pass. At the time Alberta had total prohibition while B.C. didn't. As a consequence, booze flowed from B.C. into Alberta and across to the U.S. which was also experimenting with prohibition.

The lucrative booze running attracted scores of participants, with Emilio "Emperor Pic" Picariello the largest, his powerful McLaughlin Sixes familiar on the streets of the Crowsnest communities. A big, genial man, he openly boasted that he could always put his hands on a large sum of cash. Many Crowsnest Pass residents believed that the bandits were after Emperor Pic who was rumored to be returning from Lethbridge with some $10,000 in cash to buy liquor in B.C.

The *Blairmore Enterprise*, in reporting the robbery, noted that the three bandits "...had booked passage from Lethbridge ... with the evident purpose of landing some individual supposed to have boarded the train at some point in the Pass with considerable money for transfer to the firm's headquarters...."

Since it was common knowledge to Pass residents that Emperor Pic bought massive quantities of liquor at Fernie, B.C., they easily guessed who the "individual" was and the whereabouts of the "firm's headquarters." One story states that when the confusion started, Pic tucked his money under a seat cushion then moved to another seat. One passenger is known to have used this ruse to save his money. As the *Calgary Herald* reported:

"To Mr. Donald, manager of the Alberta-British Columbia Power Company, goes the credit for out guessing the bandits. Sitting in the first class coach, Mr. Donald at first thought someone was playing a joke, but almost immediately sensed the seriousness of the situation and realizing he was carrying considerable cash and over $1,000.00 in cheques, he quickly shoved the wad in the crack in the seat and confidently waited for the command, 'Hands up.' "

Whether or not the Emperor was on the train has never been definite-

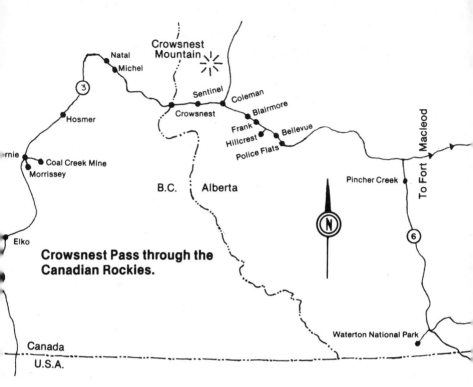

Crowsnest Mountain
Natal
Michel
Sentinel
Coleman
Crowsnest
Blairmore
Frank
Hillcrest
Bellevue
Police Flats
Hosmer
rnie
Coal Creek Mine
Morrissey
B.C.   Alberta
Pincher Creek
To Fort Macleod
Elko
Crowsnest Pass through the Canadian Rockies.
N
Canada
U.S.A.
Waterton National Park

The 60-mile- (100-km-) long Crowsnest Pass through the Rockies on the B.C.-Alberta border in the 1920s.

The Sentinel Valley in the Crowsnest Pass. Here by accident the train stopped, beginning a sequence that resulted in five deaths.

93

ly established. If he was, the robbers missed him and got only a few hundred dollars in cash, some jewelry and Conductor Jones' new $96 Elgin gold watch and chain. For Auloff, who took the watch, the consequence would prove a disaster.

Within hours of the robbery heavily-armed officers of the RCMP, CPR Police and Alberta Provincial Police had arrived in the Crowsnest. They blocked roads and searched every train and likely hiding places throughout the area. The police had learned that the three were Russians and that they had arrived in Lethbridge from Great Falls, Montana, about ten days before boarding the train. One of them, Tom Bassoff, had a glass eye which gave a glazed expression.

The first definite word of the three occurred about dusk on August 6. The accountant of the Coleman Bank of Commerce reported to RCMP Inspector Macdonald that three men answering the descriptions of the robbers had tried to cash a cheque. But when they were told they needed identification, they left.

Then early the next afternoon Joseph H. Robertson, Justice of the Peace and Coroner at Bellevue a few miles east of Coleman, was sitting at his desk. Suddenly two men stopped and glanced at a notice he had in the window. One had a glazed look in his eye.

About the same time in the nearby Alberta Provincial Police barracks Corporal Ernest Usher of the RCMP and Constables James Frewin and Frederick Bailey of the Alberta Provincials were talking. The phone rang and Corporal Usher answered it — two of the suspected bandits had been seen heading for Bellevue.

There are varying accounts of what then happened, some quite imaginative. But the unfolding tragedy didn't need embellishing. The following account, written by Corporal T. Shaw, appeared in *Scarlet and Gold*, the RCMP's quarterly magazine:

"Loading their firearms, the three set out for the eating-house, meeting the J.P. en route who also told them of the two men he had seen and that they had gone into the restaurant. The Policemen paused before entering the cafe and it was decided that Bailey would enter by the back door and Frewin and Usher by the front.

"Constable Frewin [who was in civilian clothes] walked past the booth several times where the two were eating, and deciding they were the men he told Corporal Usher. Both Policemen approached the booth with drawn revolvers.

"'Put up your hands, we are Police officers and we want you,' Frewin commanded, but instead both men dropped their utensils and let their hands fall to their sides. Frewin repeated his order, but once again it was ignored and the man he was covering began fumbling through a coat at his side and Frewin caught a glimpse of a revolver barrel coming up in the man's hand.

"Frewin shot, hitting the man in the neck, and at the same time noticed that Corporal Usher, on the right, was struggling with the other man who seemed to have a cast in his eye. Frewin fired his remaining shells at his quarry and as his gun clicked empty, Constable Bailey appeared beside him with a drawn revolver.

In the booth below, Ausby Auloff, opposite, and Constable Frewin were fatally shot and Tom Bassoff seriously wounded. The "x" marks identify bullet holes.

"Frewin, who was armed with two pistols, was apparently stunned seeing his bullets had no appreciable effect on the man he had shot, and he backed out of the door, at the same time drawing his other weapon.

"George Akoff, the wounded man, and Tom Bassoff succeeded in getting free of the booth during a scuffle with Bailey and Usher, and Joseph Robertson, the J.P. who was watching events from the middle of the street, heard a steady fusilade of shots inside the cafe. As the door opened and Frewin came out, Robertson could see Akoff and Bassoff backing Bailey and Usher toward the door, all four men firing their guns.

"Corporal Usher half turned to navigate the door and was apparently hit badly at this moment, because he collapsed at the doorstep. A second later, Constable Bailey tumbled out over top of Usher and fell to the sidewalk. Akoff next appeared at the doorway, but he just staggered along in front of the cafe, looking extremely sick, but still holding his pistol and even firing into the ground.

"Last man to come out was Bassoff with a pistol in each hand. He remained in the doorway and then, seeing Constable Bailey trying to get up, shot him through the head at point-blank range. Bailey dropped back fatally hit. Corporal Usher next attempted to struggle to his feet and this time Bassoff emptied his other gun at him and Usher lay quiet.

"Akoff and Bassoff started to cross the street and when the former had gone about 50 feet, he stiffened and slumped to the ground. Bassoff hesitated and Robertson, who also had a gun, started firing in his direction from the cover of a telephone pole. Bassoff broke into a run, turned and tried to fire, but apparently his guns were both empty so he kept jogging in the direction of the Frank slide where he eventually disappeared. He appeared to have a leg wound."

The bodies of the officers were carried to a nearby building. Six bullets had hit Usher. Bailey, unwounded in the gun battle in the cafe, had been killed by Bassoff's shot as he lay on the sidewalk.

As news of the murders spread indignant citizens joined the search, all sworn in as deputies and determined to find the wounded Bassoff and the third man, Auloff. Soon some 200 men were in the field, prepared to shoot on sight. This haste to fire would be tragic for one family.

Although it seemed impossible for the crippled Bassoff to elude capture among the massive boulders of the Frank Slide, he did. Auloff, also, seemed to have vanished. Police were puzzled over their discovery that Akoff had only one dollar on him and that after the holdup Bassoff had attempted to cash a pay cheque at Coleman. Both men were obviously short of money. Had Auloff double-crossed his companions and made off with the booty?

For two days there was no news about Bassoff, then Constable Hardy at Frank just west of Bellevue received a phone call from Mrs. Holloway who lived on a ranch 2 miles (3 km) away. "I've seen him," she said. "A big man. He was wounded. He made me give him something to eat. He threatened to come back and kill me if I told anyone he'd been here. Then he hobbled away on a stick."

The police hurried to the ranch and tightened the cordon around the area. As the *Lethbridge Herald* reported:

The Alberta Provincial Police office at Bellevue. Here the officers received the fateful call that two strangers resembling the train bandits were heading towards the community.

"The police placed implicit faith in Mrs. Holloway's story. They believed that the wounded man who visited the farm was Bassoff. Mrs. Holloway is a trained nurse and a very sensible and capable woman. She was not the least hysterical about the bandit's visit. Her story is brief and convincing, and it does not grow with telling. Though she told the bandit she did not know who he was and didn't want to know, she was sure in her own mind. She took occasion to give his leg a thorough examination. He is in bad shape.... Bassoff is therefore in such bad condition, and if he received no attention from friends since, it is possible he may be found dead...."

While the cordon was being tightened around the ranch, word came from Crowsnest to the westward that Auloff had been seen by a teamster as he was making a short-cut through the bush. The wanted man had demanded matches. He was wearing a black mackinaw with a white belt, overalls and a black sombrero, a description that fitted Auloff.

Then, from Gateway near the U.S. border, came word that a CPR brakeman had been held up at the point of a revolver as he attempted to eject a burly transient from a boxcar. Quick police work captured the suspect. He proved to be the wrong man but was jailed for carrying a concealed weapon. The chase for the bandits continued.

Wading through the rain-soaked muskeg, Constable Hidson of the Alberta Provincial Police, with Special Constable Nick Kyslik, was working his way though the gloomy woods near the small community of Crowsnest on the Alberta-B.C. border. Suddenly a deserted building loomed through the darkness. While Hidson searched the ground floor, Kyslik climbed upstairs.

Above the roar of water tumbling down the mountainside Hidson heard the rumble of an approaching train. A figure catapulted from the upstairs window and raced away. "Halt or I fire," Hidson shouted. But the figure continued to zig-zag towards the clattering boxcars.

Hidson fired and the figure pitched forward. Elbowing through the brush Hidson flashed his torch on a man crumpled on the moss. It was Special Constable Kyslik, a bullet through his heart. He left a wife and two small children.

Towards dawn the stillness of the valley was shattered by another shot which seemed to come from the vicinity of the Holloway Ranch. A rumor spread that Bassoff had committed suicide, although there was no body.

Auloff, meanwhile, appeared to be at several places at once. One report placed him near Natal, across the B.C. border. Near Waldo, also in B.C., a section foreman reported that he had seen him clambering over a barbed wire fence, leaving a piece of torn mackinaw behind. Then came what appeared to be proof that Auloff was dead.

Combing the sidehills near the B.C. border, Corporal Egan saw a piece of cloth fluttering in the wind beneath a culvert. Partly buried in the wet undergrowth lay the body of a heavily-built, mackinaw-clad man with a bullet in his back, his face so disfigured by the slashing strokes of a knife as to be unrecognizable. Egan turned to the policeman beside him. "Auloff. Tried to doublecross the others. Looks like they got even."

Later events revealed that the body was not Auloff's. He had disappeared — and so had Bassoff. In addition to the largest posses in Alberta's history, the desperate policemen brought in three bloodhounds from Seattle, complete with two U.S. police officers. Although the dogs had established a reputation for sniffing out criminals, in the Crowsnest Pass they were of no value. Heavy rains had washed out the scent.

By the fifth night of the search Bassoff was still free, despite the efforts of three police forces and some 200 citizens. On August 9 the *Calgary Herald* reported:

"According to Inspector McDonald it is thought that Bassoff is being hidden by foreign friends or being supplied with food in his hiding place in the mountains. On every pinnacle police officers with field glasses are keeping a constant lookout and investigating every suspicious movement. Every automobile is being halted and searched. . . . Police are returning after a search through the foreign section that proved fruitless.

"Details of the shooting Sunday night of Nick Kristruck [Kyslik] disclosed the fact that his partner fired the fatal shot.

" 'He was one of the most valuable men in the search,' said Inspector McDonald. 'The past three days. . .he never rested a minute. The entire countryside is aroused to a high pitch with everyone carrying rifles.' "

Then came electrifying news. Bassoff had been captured. On the evening of August 11 Tom Hammond, operating a pusher engine between Burmis and Pincher at the east end of the Crowsnest Pass, had seen a man lying near the tracks. At Lundbreck he reported to his superior and quickly left with CPR policemen on his engine. As the green lights of Pincher's yard limits came into view the officers began a new search. Constable J.S. Glover found the fugitive. He later wrote:

"I heard someone moving in a vacant lot south of the hotel, and, bending down, made out the form of a man in the darkness, and went over to see who it was. Flashing my torchlight in his face, I recognized him (from the police description) as Tom Basoff. I then covered him with my revolver and ordered him to put his hands up.

"He made no move to put his hands up, and remarked, 'You're crazy, what for I hold my hands up?' I again cautioned him to throw his hands up and upon his refusal to do so, kicked him on the right elbow with my left foot. At that he put his hands high above his head."

He carried two guns, one empty but the other loaded, and $80. Among rumpled papers was a Russian army registration number and a passport with the name Thomas Bassoff — the man who had murdered two police officers and indirectly caused the death of a third. He had also struggled nearly 40 miles (65 km) through mountainous terrain, one leg so badly smashed by a bullet that he had to limp every step with a stick for a crutch. He had eluded some 200 men and broken through the police cordon. But for Engineer Tom Hammond's vigilance, he might have obtained sanctuary among sympathizers at Macleod, less than 30 miles (50 km) away.

He was taken to the Lethbridge jail where he admitted that police had frequently been so close they could have stepped on him. To the wardens he told of meeting an old man and giving him $5 for his cap and coat, and having taken out his glass eye and put it in his pocket as a further disguise. In broken English he admitted he'd come from Russia but denied that he'd shot either of the police.

On the grey morning of October 13, Tom Bassoff faced Judge McCarthy of the Alberta Supreme Court at Macleod, charged with murder. Clad in a black mackinaw and a pair of overalls that still bore the mark of Usher's bullet, he pleaded not guilty.

But at the end of the two-day trial when the jury returned, Bassoff could see that his not guilty plea had been rejected. Without a quiver he heard himself sentenced to hang on December 22.

On that day, the shops and houses of Lethbridge glittering with festive finery, Tom Bassoff mounted the scaffold in the snow-swept courtyard. The *Lethbridge Herald* later reported:

"Just before six o'clock the sheriff went to the cell to give the word and to see that the condemned man's arms were properly bound. He was led by his guard to the scaffold which he mounted practically unaided. There was no sign of a breakdown. . . . When the trap was sprung at 6:04 this morning and Tom Bassoff, bandit, murderer, plunged into eternity at the end of the hangman's rope, the fifth life was snuffed out in the tragic chain started August 2nd last when Bassoff, Arkoff and Auloff held up CPR train No. 63 at Sentinel in Crowsnest Pass, and justice had been appeased for the murder of Corp. Usher and Constable Bailey at Bellevue August 7th."

With the execution of Bassoff the case of the three Russians appeared to have ended. Arkoff had died in the Bellevue battle; Auloff had been slain by fellow criminals he'd tried to dupe; Tom Bassoff had been hanged. But despite the certainty of Detective Egan and other officers that the body found in the Crowsnest culvert was Auloff's, Assistant Superintendent John D. Nicholson of the Alberta Provincial Police remained unconvinced.

The Alberta Attorney General gave him permission to pursue the case and on Nicholson's recommendation offered a $1,000 reward. Exchanging his uniform for civvies Nicholson boarded a train and headed south. With

Alberta's Provincial Police Assistant
Superintendent James D. Nicholson,
opposite, didn't believe that
Auloff was dead.

Below: Bellevue's Main Street in the
1920s and today. The Bellevue Cafe still
serves the public, but as a restaurant. In
the background is the Frank Slide.

brilliant detective work he proved his point, although when he wrote of the search in his book, *On the Side of the Law*, he made it sound routine:

"Gathering clues here and there, I eventually arrived in Portland, Oregon, hot on the trail. I gave what information I could to the officials of that city and also a description of the stolen watch. From there I travelled to St. Helen, Washington, where I learned that a number of Russians were working on a railway extension which was being built into the timber lands of the northern part of the state. The general foreman of the project was an acquaintance of mine. He gave me a letter of introduction to all superintendents, authorizing them to give me all possible assistance. At the fourth camp I visited (after travelling more than seventy miles on foot through rough country) I learned that Nick Bassoff, cousin of Tom Bassoff, had left camp that morning with a man answering Auloff's description.

"Crossing the Columbia River, I caught a train for Seattle and upon arriving there secured the valuable service of Detective Meteski of Seattle Police Force. Together we searched all poolrooms and taverns along the waterfront. Finally we located a brother-in-law of Auloff's. He could not or would not give us any information about the fugitive, and I returned to Edmonton very much disappointed.

"On July 18th, 1923, nearly three years after the holdup, I received a wire from the Chief Constable of the Portland Police Force, which stated that the watch in question had been found in a Portland pawnshop and was being held for identification.

"Detective Schrappe of the APP was sent to Portland from where he wired that the man who had been arrested in connection with the watch was not Auloff, but had purchased the watch at Butte from a man answering Auloff's description. Schrappe took the man to Butte where they visited the home of the man who had sold the watch.

"Sure enough, it was Auloff. At last we had caught up with him. He waived extradition and returned to Canada for trial. He was convicted on the charge of train holdup and robbery, and after pleading guilty was sentenced to seven years imprisonment at Prince Albert Penitentiary."

He never finished his sentence. After serving three years he died of silicosis.

With Auloff's death the blood-filled case was closed, although there was a sequel. Police officers from outside detachments who had taken part in the manhunt felt that more trouble in the Crowsnest was inevitable. Noted one of them:

"The operations of the army of whiskey peddlers in every Pass town is rapidly becoming a menace, but the police officers stationed there are entirely insufficient to stamp out the traffic. Fortunes are being made. . . . They work, unmolested, at all hours. There is nothing underhand with these men and they sell just as openly as in the days before prohibition made its entry into Alberta. Whiskey by the glass or bottle can be purchased openly and without fear of interruption. All that is needed is the 50 cents for each drink."

The prediction of more trouble proved accurate. As related in the next chapter, it centered around Emperor Pic whose bootlegging activities had probably started the sequence that had already resulted in five deaths.

Emperor Pic and the Girl in a Scarlet Tam

"The army of whiskey peddlars in every Pass town is rapidly becoming a menace," stated veteran policemen. Tragically, their prediction came true.

In the Crowsnest Pass of Southern Alberta the afternoon sun shone obliquely across the Rockies, picking out the frame buildings of the small mining town of Frank and the red-roofed barracks of the Alberta Provincial Police Detachment. Inside, Sergeant J.O. Scott picked up the jangling telephone and turned to Constable J. Day.

"It's Constable Lawson at Coleman. Says Emperor Pic's running a load of bootleg hootch in from the B.C. border. Just hightailed it through with two McLaughlins. Come on — we'll catch him at Blairmore."

The two officers quickly got into their car and headed towards Blairmore, another mining community a mile (1.6 km) to the west between Coleman and Frank. It was September 21, 1922, the mists of Indian summer winding gossamer scarves about the snow-crowned peaks of the Rockies above. But while the scenery was spectacular, a grey cloud of lawlessness enveloped the Crowsnest.

The cause was prohibition which had become law in Alberta in 1916. But the prohibition element, in their victorious campaign to ban the legal sale of booze, had overlooked one reality: people who liked a drink of something stronger than water were going to get it. If not legally, then otherwise. As a consequence, supplying illegal booze to willing customers became a lucrative venture with attendant corruption of officials and the deaths of several law enforcement officers.

In Southern Alberta during the province's eight-year experiment with prohibition were scores of bootleggers, with Emilio Picariello the largest. In a few years he had risen to wealth and power, earning not only the nickname "Emperor Pic" but also a seat on the Blairmore Town Council. In his powerful McLaughlin Six cars — nicknamed the "Whiskey Sixes" — he openly defied the Alberta Provincial Police and the RCMP. It was

Emilio "Emperor Pic" Picariello,
king of southern Alberta's
bootleggers, and Florence Lassandra.

the Emperor that Sergeant Scott and Corporal Day now hoped to catch with a load of illegal liquor.

"There he is," Day suddenly exclaimed as the two officers cruised down Blairmore's main street which was also the main road through the Crowsnest Pass. Beside an empty McLaughlin Special parked before the Alberta Hotel stood stocky Emperor Pic, surveying them from beneath his Homburg hat. Bringing his car to a halt, the Sergeant flashed a warrant. "I'm searching your place," he told him.

Pic honked the McLaughlin's horn. From behind the hotel came an answering toot. Another McLaughlin suddenly careened around the corner, barely missed the police car and thundered west with open throttle. At the wheel of the liquor-filled vehicle was Picariello's twenty-year-old son, Steve.

By the time the officers got into their own car to pursue Steve, Emperor Pic was already speeding down the dusty, winding road, protecting the rear of his son's vehicle. At one point Sergeant Scott took to the ditch and managed to pass the Emperor's car. But when he slowed down at the Greenhill Hotel to allow Constable Day to phone the police at Coleman, the Emperor passed him. By skillful jockeying he then prevented the police car from overtaking the fleeing McLaughlin.

About a mile from Blairmore, Scott abandoned the chase. Steve continued his high speed race for the B.C. border, while his father, the immediate danger passed, followed at a more leisurely pace.

At Coleman, warned by Chief Houghton that the cars were returning, Constable Lawson stepped to the middle of the street in an attempt to halt the boy. When Steve refused to stop, Lawson fired at him twice. Commandeering the car of William Bell, a local resident, Lawson and Houghton gave chase and fired a third shot at the speeding McLaughlin before the police car had a flat, ending the chase.

On their return to Coleman, the policemen met the senior Picariello and Constable Lawson stopped to speak to him. "You might as well bring the boy back, for if you don't I will," he said.

Emperor Pic then continued towards the B.C. border. He evidently learned that the police had shot his son, but there was no indication of the severity of the injury.

On his return to Blairmore, Emperor Pic overtook Sergeant Scott and talked good-naturedly with the police officer. According to Scott's later testimony, Pic said: "So, you didn't get the load."

Scott replied that he wasn't finished. There would be charges under the Motor Vehicle Act.

Pic replied: "I saved my load, anyway, and I don't care how many times I ditch you. It was lucky for Lawson that he did not kill my boy, or else I would kill him."

Thus began a series of events that resulted in an unarmed policeman being shot in the back and two people meeting the hangman.

The central figure in the unfolding drama was Emilio Picariello, otherwise known as the "Bottle King" and "Emperor Pic." Born in Sicily in 1875, he immigrated to Canada about 1900 and settled in Toronto. By 1911 when he moved to B.C., he had a family of seven children.

In B.C. Picariello settled in Fernie at the western end of the Crowsnest Pass and began working in a macaroni factory. A big man who weighed nearly 200 pounds (90 kg) he had a huge zest for life and an amazing capacity for work. At Fernie one of his closest friends became P. Carosella, the local wholesale liquor dealer. It was therefore not surprising that Emilio was soon in the liquor business as a local representative for the Pollock Wine Company.

In addition, he was now manager of the macaroni factory. He had also tried manufacturing cigars, had developed a large foodstuff business and in 1916 began manufacturing ice cream. He was soon producing 400 gallons a day, had put an ice-cream wagon on the streets of Fernie and opened ice-cream parlours in Blairmore, Alberta, and Trail, B.C.

As another sideline, he began to collect bottles. At first, the community merely smiled at this seeming eccentricity for Pic was well-liked. But gradually it became apparent that something was happening to the beer bottle in-

Emperor Pic's Alberta Hotel was the center of his lucrative bootlegging operation.

The powerful McLaughlin-Buick Six, nicknamed the "Whiskey Six," was Pic's favorite vehicle.

dustry. On September 22, 1916, he advertised 27,000 bottles for sale, quarts 40 cents, pints 22 cents a dozen. Unassumingly, the big, smiling man had gained a monopoly on bottles and the local breweries soon found it cheaper to rely on his efficient bottle-gathering system than to try to collect their own or buy new ones. Thereafter, his advertisement appeared regularly in newspapers throughout the Pass: "E. Pick, the Bottle King, requests that all persons selling bottles hold them until they see E. Pick, who pays top prices."

When prohibition came to Alberta in 1916, the Bottle King, as agent for the Pollock Wine Company, moved quickly into the export business and began to make money since Alberta's prohibition law at first permitted residents to import liquor. In January 1918 he purchased the Alberta Hotel in Blairmore from Fritz Sick of the Lethbridge Brewing Company and moved his family to the community.

On April 1, 1918, the Alberta government presented Pic and other bootleggers with a bonanza when total prohibition was declared. The new law meant that residents could no longer order their liquor shipped in, effectively drying up the province — at least legally. Since Southern Alberta had voted against prohibition, the majority of its citizens patronized Pic's bootlegging venture and freely gave him every cooperation.

Starting with Model T Fords, he dampened the thirst of residents of Alberta's Crowsnest Pass communities. To cope with the occasional police road barrier, he equipped his Fords with bumpers made from piping filled with concrete. He used the Alberta Hotel as a legitimate front for his rum-running activities and loved the hazards and the prestige it gave him. Towards the end of 1918 he replaced his Fords with McLaughlin Sixes, one of the most powerful cars on the road.

He also excavated a room off the basement in his Alberta Hotel and from it extended a tunnel to give access to the road. The entrance to this side room was usually covered with burlap sacking, and in front of this rough curtain were several large barrels in which were stored empty 40-ounce bottles. A favorite way of bringing in liquor was to load trucks with flour. The outer layers of sacks contained flour — in case of a search — but behind this innocent wall were burlap sacks containing bottles of illicit booze. The trucks were able to drive right under the building to deposit their dual loads. The liquor was concealed in the tunnel and the flour distributed to needy families.

One of the Emperor's prized possessions was a player piano in the hotel lounge. When played loudly, as it usually was, it nullified the noise of the activity in the basement.

As he became more affluent, he subscribed for $50,000 in Canadian Victory Bonds to help the war effort, and gave freely to the poor at Christmas. It was Emilio's boast that he could place his hands on a large sum of cash at a moment's notice. To prove his point to an old friend, Tony Andrea, he once picked up a wad of dirty rags from the floorboards of his car and unwrapped $3,000 in bills.

It was common knowledge throughout the Pass that Emperor Pic was in the rum-running business and that as a profitable and necessary sideline he bought empty bottles. The Department of the Attorney General in

Constable S.A. Lawson and, below, the Alberta Provincial Police headquarters at Coleman where he lived with his wife and five children. When he was shot in the back he fell between the house and the hospital, left.

Edmonton did an excellent business with the Bottle King in this latter respect and regularly sold him large shipments of empty beer and whiskey bottles. One recorded sale in May 1919 was for 720 dozen bottles at 40 cents a dozen.

Pic loved driving the big McLaughlin Sixes, and later the Sevens. Picking up supplies at Fernie in B.C. or his Alberta Hotel in Blairmore, he would run through the Crowsnest then veer south near Pincher Creek across the almost trackless foothills. Here, through what became known as Whiskey Gap, he would head into Montana since the U.S. now also had prohibition.

On one of these trips through Whiskey Gap he ran into a severe rainstorm which mired his whiskey-laden car. Going to a nearby house, he discovered two Alberta Provincial Police Constables on patrol who had sought shelter from the storm. After enlisting their help to free his car, he flashed his famous smile and waved a cheery goodbye. The Constables never imagined that the affable, farmerish-looking man in the sloppy blue overalls was the noted Emperor Pic. They returned to the house to await the end of the storm so that they could continue their vigil for rum runners.

There seems to have been an unwritten set of rules to the rum-running game — rules which were followed by police in some instances and by the majority of "respectable" rum runners. One of these rules was that as long as the rum runners operated like legitimate businessmen, they were not seriously molested. In this instance, "legitimate" seemed to include owning one's own equipment, refraining from violence if caught and from stealing cars for transportation. However, with the sequence of events which began in the Crowsnest Pass on September 22, 1922, the unwritten set of rules vanished.

After returning to Coleman from the unsuccessful attempt to stop Steve Picariello, Constable Lawson went to the police barracks which was also home to his wife and five young children. He took off his gun and uniform jacket and started fitting a handle into an axe-head. By now the sun had dropped behind the peaks and lights twinkled in the windows of the little hospital next door. Suddenly nine-year-old Pearl, eldest of their children, rushed in. "Daddy, there's a car outside. They want to see you."

The unarmed Lawson strode outside to a McLaughlin with two shadowy figures inside. He put his foot on the running board and began a conversation with the man at the wheel. Suddenly shots erupted from inside the vehicle. Constable Lawson turned to seek the safety of the building then collapsed. The car sped away.

Mrs. Lawson rushed out of the house and dropped beside her husband. "Oh, daddy, you're shot," she cried.

Then she saw somebody running from the hospital and, as she later testified, "I asked them to look after Mr. Lawson while I telephoned Sergeant Scott."

Nothing could be done for Constable Lawson. He had been shot in the back and was dead.

As word of the tragedy flashed through the Crowsnest Pass, residents were shocked. Why would anyone want to shoot an unarmed policeman in the back, virtually within sight of his wife and young children?

Young Pearl, who had told her father that someone was outside wanting to see him, gave Sergeant Scott the first clue. "I was waiting to go to the movies," she told him with brimming eyes. "I saw a big car driving towards the house.... Daddy walked over to the car, I saw him hold the man's arm over his head, the lady in the car fired shots and Daddy fell."

"The lady fired shots! What lady, Pearl?"

"I dunno," sobbed the girl. "Only she was wearing a scarlet tam."

Scott drove to the Alberta Hotel with Day. Here he arrested McAlpine, Pic's mechanic, on suspicion, and scoured the town for the McLaughlin. There was no sign of it. Then a phone call to Michel, across the B.C. border, brought word that Steve Picariello had run into a B.C. Provincial Police road block. He was under arrest, his load of contraband liquor seized along with the McLaughlin. One of Lawson's bullets, the B.C. officers told him, had grazed Steve's right hand but he wasn't seriously wounded.

To Sergeant Scott, as well as the officers commanding the various squads of police, there seemed little doubt that Emperor Pic, or one of his gang, had driven the murder car. But who was the woman in the red tam who, according to Pearl, had fired the shots? Though Pic had warred with the police over his trade in bootleg whiskey he'd never shown any disposition to be an assassin. On the contrary, he endeavoured to maintain amicable relations with the lawmen. During the hunt for the murdering Bassoff gang two years before he had assisted the police by transporting them around in the powerful McLaughlins which he used for his bootlegging activities.

By now detachments of police were beginning to move to the Crowsnest Pass. First a squad of B.C. Provincials under Inspector Dunwoody, then a detachment of RCMP under Inspector Bruce, and a score of Alberta Provincial Police with a pair of bloodhounds. All were determined to capture the criminals.

Sergeant Scott, meanwhile, had hurried back to Blairmore to continue his search for the murder car. At 3 a.m. he and Constable Moriarty were keeping vigil at the Alberta Hotel when there came the purr of a high-powered car.

"Sounds like a McLaughlin!" said Moriarty, heading for the back door.

A bulky car shot towards them. "Stop!" Moriarty's flashlight illuminated the scared face of Alberto Dorenzo, operator of Blairmore's taxi stand. The light also showed that the windshield had been shattered, and that the car was Picariello's.

"Get out!" snapped Moriarty. "Where'd you get that car?"

"Near a shack in the woods beyond the Cosmopolitan Hotel," came the nervous reply. "Figured I'd better bring it in."

A hasty examination showed that the windshield had been shattered by a bullet while another had sliced the speedometer and ricocheted from the engine into the floor. On the front seat lay a live .32 automatic cartridge. Sweeping the floor with his flashlight, Scott noticed a green cloth-covered button. He put it in his pocket.

"Well," Moriarty remarked, "looks like we've got the murder car all right. The birds we're after can't be far away."

At daylight Scott ordered Dorenzo to return to where he'd found the car. It had been driven over a granite ridge and hidden in the underbrush of a gully. The flinty ground produced no tracks, but as Scott searched on hands and knees he whistled. Clearly outlined on the soft moss was the print of a high-heeled shoe. So Steve's young daughter was right. Somewhere in the tragedy was a woman — a woman who, according to Pearl, had worn a scarlet tam and fired the fatal shot.

With Constable Day, Scott next searched the site where Lawson had been murdered. They picked up four discharged .32 Dominion shells similar to the one found in the car.

At noon the force was augmented by another squad under Assistant Superintendent J.D. Nicholson of the Alberta Provincial Police. After a meeting of the heads of the three forces, the posses were concentrated in a circle around the rugged terrain where the car had been abandoned.

In one search party were Constable Bradner of the B.C. Provincial Police and Constables Tutin and Clark of the RCMP. After checking every shack and cabin on the outskirts of Blairmore they decided to flush the side of a pine-clad mountain that reared above them. It was four in the afternoon, and the westering sun was already dropping behind the peaks.

They crashed through thickets, clambered up rocky escarpments and shouldered through the matted tangle of spruce. Pausing to wipe the sweat from his eyes, Clark heard a shout. Bradner was pointing to a thick-set figure that had broken from a clump of matted spruce and was clumsily scaling the slope towards the summit. Loosening their revolvers they pressed forward, gaining swiftly.

The bulky figure hauled itself upward and stood silhouetted against the sky before disappearing. The officers continued forward, working from rock to rock. Suddenly Clark lifted a warning hand. Fifty yards ahead from a clump of spruce was the glint of a rifle. "Hands up!" Bradner shouted.

A moment's silence. Then from the brush rose a haggard figure — the Emperor of Crowsnest Pass. "All right, gentlemen," he replied. "I'll surrender — I won't do you any harm."

Disarmed, he turned weary eyes on Bradner. "My son, Steve," he demanded. "Tell me — is he dead?"

"Dead!" growled Bradner. "He only got his hand scratched."

Pic's eyes lit with relief. "They phoned me from Michel that he was shot. I figured Lawson killed him. How's Lawson?" He eyed them anxiously.

"Dead!" answered Bradner curtly.

Three hours later, wrists and ankles manacled and guarded by three armed officers, Emperor Pic was on his way to jail at Lethbridge.

Meanwhile, Sergeant Scott and Day had been trying to identify the woman in the red tam. They quickly learned that Florence Lassandra, the twenty-two-year-old wife of Pic's mechanic, had driven west through the Crowsnest in a car chauffered by McAlpine shortly before the murder.

"I've a hunch that Lassandra girl's over at the Dubois house," Scott told Moriarty after a second questioning of McAlpine. "While I'm drawing her out keep your eyes open for a red tam, and a green coat that matches the button we found in Pic's McLaughlin."

At the Dubois house they were greeted with a smile from a slim, long-haired girl reclining on a sofa. Taking a cigarette from her lips she invited the officers to be seated.

Corporal McWilliams with bloodhounds and, below, Sergeant Scott searching a car during the hunt for Emperor Pic.

"I suppose," suggested Scott, "you know what brought us here?"

"I haven't the least idea."

"It's about the killing of Constable Lawson," Scott told her. "But you need not be afraid."

"He's dead and I'm alive," she laughed lightly. "I've nothing to be afraid of."

"Then slip on your coat and hat and come along."

She went into a bedroom and returned wrapped in a green cloth coat with matching toque. Casually, Scott drew from his pocket the green cloth button and placed it against her coat.

"Why," her eyes widened, "where did you pick that up — I thought I had lost it?"

"In the car Lawson was shot from," came Scott's brittle answer. "Where's the gun you packed that night?"

"Sergeant," she replied, "you've got my dad on some trumped-up charge. You've been after him for years. Don't tell me now you're trying to pin Steve Lawson's death on me!"

Scott didn't answer. Leaving her in charge of Moriarty he hurried to the house of her friend, Mrs. Gibeau. Wedged between the cushions of a couch was a fully loaded .38-calibre automatic. He returned to find that Mrs. Dubois had set a lunch and joined the girl and Moriarty at the table. Annoyed at Florence Lassandra's refusal to take the situation seriously, he arose. "Well," he said, "if you're all set we'll hit the trail for Lethbridge."

"Lethbridge!" gasped the girl, all laughter gone.

"Sure," Scott replied. "You'll be needed as a material witness."

Next day a coroner's jury returned a verdict that Lawson had died by a bullet fired by the occupants of the car in front of the detachment. Doctor Scott stated that a single notched .32 automatic bullet had struck him in the back, touched the heart and lodged beneath the skin of the right breast.

Two days later Constable Lawson was buried with military honors in his home town of Macleod which he had left during World War One to distinguish himself on the battlefields of France. His grave was near that of his comrades, Constable F. Bailey and Corporal E. Usher who had been slain at Bellevue two years before by the train robbers. As a mark of respect, in Macleod all stores and offices were closed.

Soon afterward dismay swept Pic's supporters when word reached them that he and Lassandra had been committed to appear before the Supreme Court at Calgary on November 27 to face murder charges. Steve Picariello, the dare-devil driver who had started all the trouble, was fined $100 and released.

Excitement swept the West as the day of the trial approached. Pictures of Lassandra appeared on the front pages of newspapers from coast to coast, arousing an interest in the case unequalled in decades. She entered court wearing a black dress trimmed with scarlet, waved to friends and remarked with radiant confidence: "Don't worry — I'll be with you soon." Then pushing up her long hair with a slender hand she gazed calmly about her. Less at ease, Pic hunched on his elbows, eyes on the floor.

Among the many witnesses to appear before the six-man jury during the week-long trial was nine-year-old Pearl Lawson. In a straightforward way that carried deep conviction she told how she had seen her daddy murdered. Dramatically she lifted herself on tip-toe and pointed a small accusing finger at Florence Lassandra. "That's the lady," she said, "who shot my daddy!"

While Pearl was led away weeping, Sergeant Scott rose. He delivered one damning piece of evidence after the other to back up the Crown's claim that Florence Lassandra was "the lady in the red tam" whom Pearl had seen fire the fatal shot at her father. A red tam found in her room along with five .32 Dominion cartridge shells were produced as evidence, along with a loaded .38 automatic she admitted leaving wedged between the cushions at Mrs. Gibeau's.

While Florence sat, her poise shattered, the Sergeant read the statement she'd given police. Pic had received a telephone call saying that Lawson had shot his son. Beside himself with anger, convinced that his son was dead, Pic had leapt into his car and, with Florence beside him, driven to Coleman barracks. Calling Lawson out, he asked where his son was.

"Lawson said he didn't know," Scott read. "Then Pic said 'You're going with me to find him — you shot him.' Lawson said 'What of it!' Then I heard two shots. One grazed my leg and the other broke the windshield. Pic was struggling with Lawson so he couldn't have fired them. Then I guess I got scared and must've started shooting. I fired a couple of shots in the air, but someone else shot Lawson."

Scott surveyed the court. "It was her own bullets, not those of Lawson or anyone else, that smashed the windshield and speedometer," he stated. "I traced the lines of trajectory. The bullets could only have come from a person seated inside the car on the far side of the front seat. And," he paused, "the empty shells found at the murder spot were identical with those I discovered in Florence Lassandra's bedroom. When Lawson was shot even his tunic was in the barracks and his revolver hanging in the office — empty!"

T.F. Brown of Blairmore testified that on the evening of the murder he had met Pic in a state of great excitement and heard him swear: "If any Constable has shot my boy, I'll kill him tonight, by God!" Then Pic had kissed his gun and driven towards Coleman.

The trial was completed on Friday night and as *The Morning Albertan* reported:

"...Mr. Justice Walsh, the trial judge, said that in view of the importance of the case, he would adjourn court until 2 o'clock Saturday afternoon. He told the jury that his summing up would occupy about one hour and a half and that they probably would enter upon their deliberations by 3:30 Saturday afternoon.

"It was with great difficulty that the large crowds attending the Friday session of the trial were kept from swarming into the court room. All day long the corridors were thronged with morbid curiosity seekers. Scores who were unable to gain admittance into the court room for the morning session waited in line until noon, and when the noon session was called they swarmed in. This procedure was repeated at the evening session. The provincial police officers formed a cordon to keep the crowds at a distance and when the court room was comfortably filled all doors were locked and those who could not get in were asked to leave the building.''

The case had attracted so much attention that when the jury returned its verdict the paper reported the news in a special edition. Across the front page was a massive two-word headline: "BOTH GUILTY!"

Justice Walsh sentenced them to hang at Fort Saskatchewan Penitentiary near Edmonton on February 21, 1923. Florence collapsed while Pic was led away with unseeing eyes and stumbling feet.

As the winter days passed the dethroned Emperor fought to establish his innocence. Taking comfort in the assurance that it was an unwritten law in Canada that no woman should be hanged, and that a quarter of a century had elapsed since a woman had gone to the scaffold, Florence joked with her guards. She was confident that her death sentence would be commuted.

This belief in her immunity brought an idea to Florence. If she confessed to the accidental shooting of Lawson, and admitted Pic's complete innocence, he'd be released — free to exert his wealth and political connections to free her, too.

Buoyed by this conviction she signed a confession and smilingly awaited word of Pic's release. But the days slipped by until the shadow of the noose was only a week away. Then came word that an appeal had been granted. Florence was exultant. Her plan had worked. But soaring hopes were shattered when a Judge confirmed the death sentences on the grounds that both were in the murder car and equally involved.

But Florence still clung to the assurances of lawyers and friends that

In Blairmore, Emperor Pic's hotel is still in use, although remodelled as a drugstore. The remains of the tunnel are still in the basement.

there would be a last minute reprieve. It was a view shared by the public who felt that the girl had made a sporting attempt to sacrifice herself to save Pic, but she had been doublecrossed. Throughout the West, women's organizations bombarded the Minister of Justice with petitions for a reprieve. By May 1, however, the shadow of the gallows only twenty-four hours away, there was still no word of clemency.

Both went to their deaths on the morning of May 2. A special dispatch from Fort Saskatchewan to the Calgary *Herald* provided details:

"Within the high forbidding walls of the jail here, in the gloomy dawn, with low clouds scudding across a fretful morning sky, Mary Florence Lassandra today followed Emilio Picariello to the scaffold. The sun had scarce risen above the horizon when the last chapter in Alberta's most fateful bootlegging tragedy had been written, and the law was avenged for the slaying of its officer, Constable Steve Lawson, at Coleman last September.

"Dawn had just begun faintly to illuminate the eastern sky when the little solemn group of jail officials approached the death cell where Picariello has lain for the past four months. The door clanged open to the prisoner for the last time. Preceded by Warden Griggs and Sheriff Rae, with three guards, and accompanied by Father Fidelis, Franciscan monk and priest of the little parish church here, Picariello walked with unfaltering steps to the scaffold.

"As Hangman Wakefield stepped up to him to put the black cap on him, Picariello growled: 'Take that accursed thing away. I can face what's ahead with my eyes open.'

"It was explained that the law insisted that the black cap must be worn, and the request was refused.

" 'You are hanging an innocent man, God help me,' said Picariello, as he stepped upon the trap. It was then exactly fifteen minutes after five.

"Ten minutes later the body was removed.

"Mrs. Lassandra followed Picariello to the scaffold within the hour. It had been a series of tragic followings for Florence Lassandra since she followed Picariello into the lucrative bypaths of whiskey-running across the British Columbia border in the Crow's Nest. She followed Picariello into the death car when they made their mad dash of revenge into Coleman that ended in the slaying of Constable Steve Lawson.

"Mrs. Lassandra had spent the night in prayer with the priest. She ate no breakfast, contrasting with the bacon and eggs, toast and coffee that Picariello ate with equanimity just before the death summons.

"With firm step Florence Lassandra began the long walk from the women's building, across the jail yard, and to the gateway to eternity. She faltered for an instant as the grim scaffold was reached. The liquid notes of a robin suddenly and startlingly poured into the gloom of the morning, a draft of hope.

" 'Why do they hang me when I didn't do anything?' she asked the little group at the foot of the scaffold. 'Is there no one here who's got any sympathy for me? I forgive everybody.'

"Eleven minutes later the body was removed."

The Yukon's Christmas Day Assassins

In the Yukon's most brutal crime three men were murdered, then snow covered the evidence. But brilliant sleuthing by Detective Harry Maguire and NWMP Constable Alex Pennycuick re-created the atrocity to a jury's satisfaction.

Lower Lake Laberge, a typical NWMP Post during the Klondike gold rush. In trying to avoid such a Post, O'Brien brought suspicion on himself.

With a fat Canada goose sizzling in the oven, Corporal Patrick Ryan of the North-West Mounted Police's Hootchikoo Detachment jerked open the door for the third time that Christmas night. He gazed impatiently across the moon-drenched surface of the Yukon River but failed to see any dark figure moving against the violet-tinted snowdrifts. He had invited telegraph lineman Ole Olsen to share his Christmas dinner but there was no sign of him. "Guess he's run into a bunch at Fussell's roadhouse and the boys are whooping it up," he thought as he closed the door. But still he wondered.

Ole Olsen wasn't the type of person to casually break a promise.

It was the closing week of 1899. At Dawson City, 50 miles (80 km) to the northward, miners were fighting the frozen creeks in their search for gold — creeks which since the Klondike stampede of 1898 had already yielded gold by the hundreds of tons. While most of the 50,000 or so men who had trekked north the previous year were honest, a few came to mine not the gravel but those who had wrested the gold from its frozen bed.

To help protect the miners who had struck pay gravel then ventured along the 400-mile (640-km) wilderness trail to Skagway where boats connected to Vancouver and Seattle, NWMP Superintendent Sam Steele had increased the strength of the force in the Yukon. Now 10 officers and over 230 scarlet-coated men patrolled the silent reaches, their duties ranging from collecting customs dues to slashing trails, controlling the honky-tonks in Dawson City to protecting miners from the criminal element. To further

ensure the safety of those travelling through the frozen wilderness, the resourceful Sam Steele had scattered detachments along the route.

There was Fort Selkirk, 170 miles (275 km) south of Dawson; then Minto 18 miles (29 km) farther on; Hootchikoo, 16 miles (26 km) beyond and, at an equal distance, Five Fingers, and so the chain of police posts continued right to the Alaska border. It made miners packing thousands of dollars of yellow gold dust feel safer to realize that the trail was under the vigilance of these Mounted Police. Without them they would be entirely at the mercy of the human vultures who, despite all attempts to keep them out, had found their way into the gold camps.

As a further means of keeping in closer touch, the Mounted Police had just completed a frontier telegraph line between Dawson and the Alaska boundary. It was a rough affair, strung from tree to tree, and Ole Olsen and his fellow linemen were kept busy freeing the line of fallen trees and other debris that encumbered it after every thaw or blizzard.

Ole never did appear at Corporal Ryan's that Christmas Day. By December 31 he was still missing and Ryan was getting anxious. Restlessly, he again glanced over a report he had received from Constable Alexander Pennycuick of Fort Selkirk Detachment. It referred to two undesirables named Tom Miller and Charlie Ross who had robbed an ice-locked scow at Hell's Gates and were said to be hiking southward.

Well, it was a cinch they hadn't passed through Hootchikoo or he would have see them. They must still be somewhere between Hootchikoo and Fort Selkirk. All he could do was watch for them. Then his thoughts swung to the missing lineman. Had Ole met with an accident or had the Christmas thaw given him extra work? Corporal Ryan decided to investigate.

Slipping on his parka and worming his moccasined feet into snowshoe thongs, he crunched over the crusted drifts towards Minto, eyes alert. The Christmas thaw and subsequent bitter cold had crusted the snow but there had since been another storm.

At a point where a cut-off known as the "Pork Trail" led through the woods he hesitated. The Pork Trail had been slashed by freighters hauling supplies to Dawson to avoid a wide bend in the river and the telegraph line followed it. Ryan decided to take it, hoping to find some clue to Ole's inexplicable absence. He had covered some 9 miles (14 km) when a slight depression, running at right angles to the trail, caught his eye. It might have been an animal path, but looked much more like a snowed-in trail made by human feet. He decided to investigate.

For twenty minutes he walked parallel with the depression, careful not to disturb it, then suddenly stopped. Before him an abandoned tent arose from a wall of unbarked logs. The absence of animal stretchers told him that it was not a trapper's. Why, then, a tent so far from the beaten track? His eyes took a swift inventory as he stepped in. The bunk was large enough for two men. Suddenly he tensed. Piled in a corner were sacks and boxes of provisions — each bearing the mark of the trading company whose goods had been pilfered from the scow at Hell's Gates. He had stumbled on Miller and Ross's hangout! Quickly he listed the contents of the tent. Then, stepping out into the snow, he made his way thoughtfully back towards the Pork Trail.

Darkness had settled upon the woods when he at last reached the long ebony rectangle of Captain Fussell's roadhouse, broken by orange squares of light that shone cheerily on the purple drifts. From the stovepipe a white column of vapour rose into the bejewelled sky. From the ice on his parka Ryan realized it must be nearly -60°F (-50°C).

Throwing open the door he entered and shook hands with Captain Fussell. Dropping into a babiche-netted chair before the red hot box-stove he listened to the Captain's account of the latest up-river gossip.

"Say, Fussell," Ryan eyed the tall, rawboned figure anxiously, "what happened to Ole Olsen? He was due at my place for dinner on Christmas Day, but hasn't shown up yet."

"What!" Fussell's jaw sagged. "That's damned queer. Ole left here early Christmas morning. Couldn't keep him. Said you'd be waiting dinner for him."

Ryan frowned. "Was he alone?"

"No. Two men from Dawson bunked here the night afore. Fred Clayson, a fellow from Seattle who'd struck it rich on the creeks, and another guy named Lynn Relfe, caller-off in one of the dance-halls. They were on their way outside with quite a pile. Figgered on spendin' Christmas here only Ole was so anxious to keep that date with you they decided to pull out with him. Don't tell me you didn't see them!"

"Neither one of them. Think I'll hike back to Five Fingers in the morning. Maybe Sergeant Parker'll know something. Give me a sheet of paper, I want to drop a line to Alex Pennycuick at Fort Selkirk. Guess you can find someone to take it over."

Late the following evening Ryan shook off his snowshoes, entered the low log barracks at Five Fingers and clasped the sinewy hand of Sergeant Parker. Through the frosty air boomed the menacing roar of the nearby rapids, mingling with the companionable crackling of the red-hot stove. Ryan gazed anxiously about the white-painted living-room for a sign of the missing Olsen; a glance that wasn't lost on Parker.

"Well, Corporal, what's eating you?" he asked.

"Have you seen Olsen? He left Fussell's early Christmas morning for my place and seems to have disappeared. Figured he might be here."

"Haven't seen him since the 21st," Parker answered with obvious surprise. "Constable Buxton came back on the 24th with all Olsen's tools except his pliers and file. Fact is, Ryan, I've been worried myself. It was pretty soft on Christmas Day and I've a hunch he hit a bad spot and went through. This Yukon's treacherous. Solid ice one day, shell ice the next. All depending on the current. Too bad if he got drowned."

Ryan's eyes narrowed. "But don't forget, he was travelling with Relfe and Clayson and ... between them they were packing a tidy amount of coin. Guess I'll have a bite and hit the hay. I'm meeting Pennycuick on the Pork Trail at noon tomorrow."

With growing apprehension Ryan returned to his detachment at Hootchikoo next morning and continued until he came to the Pork Trail. Fresh tracks showed that Pennycuick was there ahead of him. Then, through the frost-rimmed willows, he espied the tall angular form of the Englishman near the tent.

Above: Fred Clayson was one of three men George O'Brien helped to murder. O'Brien, at right, is shown outside the log police post after his arrest.

Corporal Patrick Ryan, below, waited for a Christmas guest who never arrived.

"Hello, Ryan," he laughed, "I've just been poking around this tent you found. It's Miller and Ross's hide-out all right. Here — look at these draught holes," he pointed to the stovepipe, "they form a perfect figure eight. Saw those same pipes and stove in Miller's camp at Hell's Gates on December 11th. Three days later, when I returned with a warrant, they'd vamoosed. Here's something else I found." On a rough spruce table were a 40.82 rifle, a bag of cartridges, a pair of pliers and a file.

"Pennycuick," announced Ryan grimly, "those pliers belong to Ole. We've got more than a scow robbery on our hands. This looks like murder."

That night word of the discovery was flashed to Dawson and Tagish. Promptly the whole Force snapped into action. Alert eyes scrutinized every traveller mushing along the icy trail towards the Alaska boundary for men answering the description of Miller and his partner.

The following day Staff Sergeant George M. Graham was gazing through the frosted windows of the Tagish barracks, near the Alaska boundary, at the most stupid piece of foolhardiness he had witnessed in many a day. A fur-coated man in a sled was whipping a team of black horses furiously across the river towards an area where the swift current undercut the ice. The driver had swerved aside from the regular trail which passed the barracks and was making directly for the dangerous ice. Behind him loped a magnificent St. Bernard dog.

"There's one bird who doesn't place much value on his hide," Graham said to Constable Thomas A. Dickson who was writing at a nearby table. "Better slip over to the stable and grab a rope — we're going to need it in a minute. Look how that ice is sagging! There! I told you. One of his horses is through. Come on. Quick."

Ploughing through the loose snow they saw that one horse was partly submerged while the other animal was thrashing frenziedly about. The driver, a heavy-set, beetle-browed man, was flailing the fear-maddened animals mercilessly with his whip.

Snatching the whip from the driver's hand, Graham swept him angrily aside. "What's the big idea abusing these beasts?" he shouted. "Here, grab this rope and help get 'em on good ice.

They got the team on to safe ice then to the barracks. Here Graham turned furiously on the big man. "What in hell possessed you to drive into that mess? Any cheechako would know better. What's your name anyway?"

"George O'Brien," he mumbled gruffly.

Graham eyed him coldly. This O'Brien had shown a suspicious anxiety to avoid contact with the police. A swift, appraising glance had already shown a Police robe on the sled. How had it come into his possession? Police equipment wasn't bartered about the country.

While O'Brien changed his wet clothes Graham questioned him about the robe. Shifty-eyed and sullen, he explained that he'd obtained it from the Officer Commanding at Dawson some time before. Then, attired once more in dry clothing, O'Brien sought the entertainment afforded by the notorious Indian Jenny in her cabin not far away.

Graham thoughtfully watched the stocky figure disappear in a world of spinning flakes, then scribbled a telegram to Inspector William Scarth at Dawson.

The Yukon River looking upstream from where the three bodies were pushed through the ice.

The Alaska Commercial, a Yukon gold-rush trail typical of the one on which Ole and his companions were shot.

A few hours later he received a reply. O'Brien's story was correct. Disgustedly, he tossed the wire to Dickson. "Guess we can pass O'Brien up. Thought we'd landed a suspect, but Dawson says his story about the robe's okay."

Shortly afterward, however, the operator entered with another telegram. It caused the Sergeant to smile and sent him ploughing through the storm. Entering the squalid cabin of Indian Jenny, he met the steely challenge in the eyes of the half-drunken O'Brien.

"O'Brien, alias Tom Miller," he snapped, "I arrest you for that scow

The frame of the tent where the assassins burned clothing and other effects of the murdered men.

robbery at Hell's Gates last December. Throw on your coat. And what happened to Graves — that partner of yours who's been calling himself Ross? Did time with you in Dawson."

"Miller!" O'Brien laughed hoarsely. "Who in hell's Miller? My name's O'Brien. I don't know nothing about your scow."

While O'Brien cursed in the guardhouse Graham and Dickson searched his sled. It contained a .30.30 Winchester, a supply of ammunition, two revolvers, two empty shells for a .41 Winchester revolver and a telescope. On the floor was a dark stain which might have been made by animal or human blood.

As he re-read the last telegram from Dawson, Graham chuckled. So closely had his description of O'Brien matched Miller's, as given in Pennycuick's report, that Inspector Scarth had had second thoughts and wired him to charge him with the scow theft. A hurried check had disclosed that O'Brien and a man named Graves had been released from Dawson jail that fall. O'Brien, destitute of funds, had been given sufficient rations to take him out of town.

Graham pondered. How, then, had he secured sufficient money since to buy a good team and all the other equipment? The Sergeant flashed another wire to Dawson. Scarth replied that he was hurrying south by dog team, bringing with him Harry Maguire, a former Pinkerton detective.

Meanwhile, Pennycuick was continuing his investigations in the vicinity of the Pork Trail. Somewhere in the area, he felt convinced, lay the answer to the mystery of the missing men. Quiet and unassuming, Pennycuick believed in employing what he termed common sense. And that common sense told him that the Christmas thaw would, as a result of the subsequent cold snap and crusting snow, leave a permanent record of what had happened that day. All he had to do was find the place of the crime and remove the new snow.

A careful survey disclosed signs of someone having climbed the sloping bank at the point where the tent trail reached the river. Then he noticed something that had previously escaped him. From the river to the tent branches had been lopped from trees and some chopped down. But why? Certainly not to clear the trail for they were cut an arm's length overhead.

Turning, Pennycuick gazed southward through the slashed bush from a hillock behind the tent. It provided a perfect view of some 10 miles (16 km) of the frozen Yukon! Now he understood the significance of that telescope found on O'Brien's sled. From this hidden tent a man with a telescope could watch, unseen, anyone following the river trail. To Pennycuick the discovery was alarming.

Leaving the knoll he examined some of the fallen trees. Each had been cut with an axe that had three distinct notches in the blade. Following the tent trail back to the river bank Pennycuick swept away the loose snow with some spruce boughs, disclosing a furrow in the crusted snow which could have been made by dragging a body over it while the snow was melting. It led to a hole in the ice which had frozen over. Picking up a tuft of yellow hair which might have belonged to O'Brien's St. Bernard he slipped it in his pocket. Then, following the furrow to the top of the bank, he found himself standing in a small snow-covered clearing ringed with frosted bushes.

Had Clayson, Relfe and Olsen, he wondered, as they swung southward that balmy Christmas morning, been enticed from the river and ambushed near this spot? To Detective Maguire, who had replaced Corporal Ryan, he confided his suspicions, then hurried to Fort Selkirk to confer with Inspector Scarth.

Scarth was worried and anxious. George O'Brien, arrogant and angry, was demanding his release. Not a shred of direct evidence had been produced to justify him being confined. And now the moccasin telegraph had brought word that Clayson and Olsen had followed a rush to a new gold strike on the Big Salmon and were working claims. It looked very much as though the police case was going to disintegrate. O'Brien could not be held indefinitely without direct evidence to connect him either with the robbery or the murder.

When Pennycuick and Maguire returned to the cut-off on the Pork Trail they brought along O'Brien's big St. Bernard. Unleashing the animal a short distance from the tent trail, Pennycuick put into effect an experiment.

"Go home!" he ordered. The St. Bernard wagged his tail, gazed questioningly at him, then lay down on the snow. "Go home!" Again Pennycuick repeated his command.

Slowly the dog arose, surveyed him for a moment, then trotted off. At the junction of the trails he swung north towards the tent. Half an hour later they found him snuggled within, obviously at home!

Maguire laughed understandingly. "Well, Pennycuick, if that doesn't tell its own story I'll eat my hat. O'Brien's up to his neck in this. It's just a case of rounding up evidence. I don't believe Clayson and Olsen were ever near the Big Salmon. Come along and I'll show you why."

Through the snow-covered spruce they crunched southward to the opening in the woods that Pennycuick had thought a likely place for an ambush. For a considerable distance around Maguire had painstakingly removed the soft snow down to the glazed surface.

Clutching the Constable's arm he pointed. Two dark red splotches stained the snow's surface. Some distance away were four more ominous stains. Frozen pools of blood!

Pennycuick nodded. "Just as I thought. Those men were seen from the tent, lured into an ambush and murdered. Then their bodies were dragged to the river and shoved through the ice. Guess the killers figured they'd be carried down to the sea, or crushed to pieces at break-up. Still — we've got to get evidence to satisfy a jury, and Yukon juries are hard-boiled. Let's give this clearing the once-over then we'll examine the snow around the tent."

Day after day, in the biting cold of -50°F (-45.6°C), they searched. On hands and knees they sifted the freezing snow through icy fingers. Gradually, painstakingly, evidence unfolded. A careful examination of every tree disclosed bullet-scarred bark and clipped-off branches. With Maguire's help Pennycuick calculated the angles of trajectory and the points from which the shooting had been done. To the mounting pile of evidence were added some splinters of bone, human hair, a 40.82 shell, a watch that had stopped at 9.02, part of a tooth broken from the root, and part of another gold-filled tooth smeared with the lead of a bullet.

At last they moved back to the tent. Standing at the doorway Pennycuick surveyed the unbroken surface of the snow.

"Mac, if you'd done away with anyone, and wished to get rid of incriminating articles you couldn't burn, what would you do?"

Maguire thought for a moment. "I'd throw 'em away — scatter 'em about."

"Exactly!" Diving his hand into his pocket Pennycuick produced a few coins, a pocket-knife and a key. With quick jerks he sent them spinning across the snow. Then with a stick he marked a semicircle outside the farthest point where they had dropped and picked up the broom. "Come

In August 1901 *The Daily Klondike Nugget* brought out a special edition on the O'Brien murders. Included among sketches in the paper were these three of Detective Maguire, above right; Constable Pennycuick, top; and Bruce, the big St. Bernard.

on, Mac, we'll sweep up all the loose snow inside this line and sift it."

Again they went to work. The results surpassed the Constable's expectations. First they discovered a lineman's leather belt, then a key, an axe with three notches in the blade that corresponded with the cuttings on the trees, a peculiar coin which Relfe was known to have carried as a charm and, finally, the charred embers of a fire. Among the ashes were remnants of burned clothing, some buttons bearing the name of a Seattle clothier, and eyelets from a pair of factory-made moccasins. Finally, from a shovelful of soft snow Penycuick withdrew a ragged scrap of paper and whistled softly. It was Ole Olsen's receipt from Fussell's roadhouse for breakfast — and it was dated Christmas morning!

Unfortunately, the most necessary evidence for a murder trial was still lacking. Despite the fact that Scarth had sent parties to cut and dynamite the river ice and drag the bottom, no bodies had been found. O'Brien, resolute and angry, was demanding his release.

At last, with a thunderous roar, the Yukon cast aside its icy fetters. Millions of tons of ice reared and leapt and went towards the sea. There seemed little hope of finding any frail human bodies after that massive force had expended itself. Nevertheless, Mounted Police patrols pushed out in canoes and commenced a systematic search of sloughs and sandbars.

On May 30 the citizens of Dawson were electrified with the news that a bullet-ridden body, identified as Clayson's, had been found on a sandbar near Fort Selkirk.

On June 11 another body was found floating down-river. In the vest pocket were visiting cards bearing the name Lynn Relfe. Sixteen days later the Yukon was brought to a still higher pitch of tension by the discovery of Ole Olsen's body on a sandbar. Each body was riddled with three or four bullets, proving that the shooting had been wild, while Olsen's skull had been crushed in. The bodies were shipped to Dawson where it was found that the two broken teeth discovered near the tent trail exactly fitted roots in the gums of Relfe and Clayson.

On the sweltering day of June 10 nearly a year later, O'Brien's trial opened in the log courthouse at Dawson City. From the dock the prisoner, self-possessed and aggressive, glowered upon the crowd of miners, gamblers and flashy women from the honky-tonks. Grimly a jury of miners and merchants awaited the testimony of eighty witnesses it had taken many months to assemble from all parts of the continent. Upon a table were piled exhibits which almost exhausted the alphabet, including tree stumps showing three notches, the notched axe itself, analyst's reports on the stains found in the snow and on the floor of O'Brien's sled, two broken teeth smeared with the lead of bullets, and the key found near the tent which had been found to fit Clayson's safe in Seattle.

Slowly the story unfolded. O'Brien and Graves had met in the Dawson jail. O'Brien had first propositioned a fellow convict named Williams, then another named Sutton, with the suggestion that when released they camp at some isolated spot, watch for gold-burdened miners, rob and kill them, and push their bodies through the ice. The swift current of the Yukon would do the rest. Both had received the proposition coldly, but Graves had succumbed to the hypnotism of O'Brien's wily tongue.

The above photo indicates the intense interest in the O'Brien case. During the trial spectators jammed doors and windows of Dawson City's courthouse.

Their time served, the Police had furnished them with an axe, a stove and some provisions. On December 12 O'Brien and Graves had stopped at Fussell's roadhouse. Four days later O'Brien had stood guard while Graves carried their purloined supplies from the Arctic Express Company's ice-locked scow into the bush; then both had disappeared. On December 26 Fussell had observed smoke rising in silvery clouds above the tree-tops in the direction in which the tent was subsequently located — and wondered. Next day O'Brien had emerged unexpectedly from the willows fringing the Pork Trail and followed a Mr. and Mrs. Prater south along the river trail towards Tagish. One night he'd been seen counting a large roll of greenbacks. On another night he'd displayed a peculiar gold nugget — the corners bent over almost like fingers clasping a small nugget within — which had formerly belonged to Relfe.

Breathlessly the jury and spectators listened as Pennycuick and Maguire filled in the details of what had happened on that tragic Christmas Day.

Between December 17 and 24 Graves and O'Brien had packed the stolen supplies to their rendezvous in the woods, cleared an aisle through the forest with the notched axe and prepared the death-trap. Through the telescope they'd watched three travellers moving southward on Christmas morning. They'd hurried down the tent trail and prepared their ambush. Below the bank they could hear the men talking and laughing as they swung along.

Suddenly Graves had appeared on the ice with his 40.82. Frightened, the men scrambled up the bank and dug for cover, only to be met with a fusillade of shots from O'Brien's .30.30. Confused by the unexpectedness of the attack the three then milled around. O'Brien and Graves were shooting wildly. Clayson dropped sixteen feet from the bank. Lynn Relfe sprang for cover; a bullet tore through his cheek, clipping out a goldfilled tooth; another found his brain. Olsen, wounded, struggled for the woods, to be overtaken and bludgeoned to death.

Coats were stripped from the bodies and thoroughly searched. A hole was cut in the ice and the victims consigned to the chilly clutches of the Yukon. Having obliterated, as they thought, all signs of the struggle, O'Brien and Graves then kindled a fire outside the tent and attempted to destroy the remaining evidence.

Prosecuting Attorney F.C. Wade, Q.C., wove one piece of evidence into another, cementing them with the exhibits. It was the ninth day of the trial and O'Brien, stolid up to this time, gazed with lowering face about him. Sergeant Graham testified to finding two bills sewn into the soles of O'Brien's boots and an additional $2,000 secreted between the runners and the iron shoeing of the sled taken from him at Tagish.

In a brilliant defence O'Brien's lawyer attempted to sweep aside the evidence as purely circumstantial. Something more than flimsy allegations were necessary when a man's life was at stake, he thundered. Wade rose to his feet.

"Your Honour, permit me to produce Quartermaster-Sergeant Telford."

When the red-coated Sergeant entered the witness-box, the prosecuting attorney passed the notched axe over. "Sergeant, do you recognize this axe?"

"Yes, sir. When O'Brien's time was up I returned his sled, dog, tent and revolver, but couldn't find an axe, so I gave him this one with a sort of apology for the three nicks. I'd know it anywhere.'

The last witness, extradited from Seattle where he had been serving a term of imprisonment, was known as the "Clear Kid" around the Dawson dance-halls, his actual name being West.

In a peculiar medley of Bowery jargon and Northern slang, ex-Faro dealer West told of occupying the cell behind O'Brien the previous winter and of being approached by him to kill and rob passing miners "to clean up a bunch o' coin" and then to "chuck their bodies in the drink." Preferring petty larceny to murder he'd refused, gone his own way and promptly landed in jail again.

At dawn on the morning of August 23, 1901, O'Brien mounted the scaffold in the barracks yard at Dawson City. Swaggering and unrepentant he dropped to his doom.

Graves, alias Ross, was never seen again. But late that summer a decomposed and bullet-riddled body was found on a sandbar far down the Yukon River. After the murders O'Brien had obviously shot his partner and pushed him through the ice to dispose of the only living testimony to his guilt. Unfortunately, in his murderous planning he had failed to include Detective Maguire, Constable Pennycuick, and the other red-coated policemen who had so brilliantly amassed the evidence that led to the gallows.

Horror on the Reserve

Two B.C. policemen had vanished. Their fate was so ghastly that investigating officers had difficulty believing the evidence.

A tree prevented the death car from being pushed into the Nicola River.

Gate at the entrance to Canford Reserve. Constable Carr stopped the car here while Gisbourne went towards the buildings where the fight started.

On May 23, 1934, Constable Percy Carr of the B.C. Provincial Police at Merritt sat down to breakfast in his cottage behind the courthouse and lockup. Afterwards, he would complete a case that would leave him free to take his family on an outing on the Victoria Day weekend. He and his wife were discussing plans for the holiday when the phone rang.

It was from the Canford Reserve, about 12 miles (20 km) away, where a band of Nuaitch Indians under Chief Billy did a little farming and ranching. The informant said that there had been a party and that Eneas George had stabbed his wife who was now in desperate need of medical attention. Carr replied that he would leave at once. He called Dr. Gillis and after picking him up hurried to the reserve.

On the drive Carr reviewed his knowledge of the George family. His thoughts were not reassuring. They were notorious troublemakers, addicted to excessive use of rotgut liquor.

Carr knew Eneas well. Some time before, under the influence of liquor, Eneas had swung an axe at him. The keen blade slashed the Constable's hat, narrowly missing his head and face. Carr had subdued Eneas without violence and sent him home. When Eneas sobered he made profuse apologies. The Constable warned him to be careful of liquor in the future or it would lead to serious trouble — a warning that was tragically prophetic.

On arrival at the reserve, Carr went to look for Eneas George while the doctor tended the injured woman. She had been stabbed in half a dozen places and was weak from loss of blood. She said that Eneas had been drinking and attacked her without provocation. He also threatened to kill her when he returned.

Carr could not locate Eneas, but did find Richardson George, a brother of the wanted man.

"Where is Eneas?" Carr asked.

"Eneas went away for a little while. He will be back tonight," was the reply.

Carr nodded. He knew it would be futile to question Richardson. The easiest way to handle this matter was to accept it as an everyday occurrence. By so doing, no suspicions would be aroused and it would be a simple matter to effect an arrest later. Any other method would arouse instant hostility. Carr told Richardson that Eneas, being a man of his word, would undoubtedly be back. When Eneas did return, he would like to see him.

Having disposed of this ticklish point, Carr then chatted amicably with Richardson and gave him the impression that Eneas would have little trouble in explaining the stabbing. It might, he said, result in Eneas receiving a sixty- or ninety-day sentence for common assault. The Indian Agent, however, would have to look into the matter as he wouldn't like Eneas stabbing his wife whenever it suited him. Richardson agreed and said that Eneas would call when he returned. With that, Carr left him.

The wounded woman was then taken to Merritt hospital. Carr made out a report for Dominion Constable Frank Gisbourne, who usually attended to problems on the reserve. But because he was in Kamloops on business it became Carr's duty.

Carr's work kept him busy all day and it was nine in the evening that he arrived home. As he was about to begin his meal, Constable Gisbourne arrived. He got to the point at once.

"I'd like you to come out to the reserve with me and pick up Eneas, Percy."

"Why, do you expect trouble?" Carr asked.

"No, but Eneas might be drunk, and I'd like to have you with me."

Carr laid down his knife and fork. He donned his tunic and started for the door.

"Aren't you going to take your gun, Percy?" Mrs. Carr asked, nodding towards the Constable's revolver hanging on the back of the chair.

"No, I'll leave it there," Carr replied.

The two officers left at once.

The next morning a bright sun gave promise of glorious holiday weather. Mrs. Carr went about her kitchen work. Though her husband had not yet returned she felt no anxiety. He had a prisoner in the cells at the courthouse, and usually slept on a cot in the cell-room when he had anyone locked up. She could see the window of the room her husband slept in from her kitchen window.

At 10 o'clock Carr had not yet appeared to get the prisoner's breakfast. Mrs. Carr thought this unusual as it wasn't like her husband to leave a prisoner without attention. She walked across to the lockup and peered in the room. Her husband's bed had not been slept in.

Mrs. Carr became uneasy. She called the post office at Canford and asked if anyone had seen the officers. Receiving a negative reply, she then called Mrs. Gisbourne.

"I haven't seen or heard of Frank since he went out last night to bring in an Indian prisoner. I'm becoming worried about him," was Mrs. Gisbourne's reply.

For the first time since her husband left, Mrs. Carr began to fear for his safety. She called Indian Agent Barber, who said he would go to Canford at once and make inquiries.

When Barber walked through the gate at the reserve he noticed blood-stains on the ground. He also saw a fresh hide thrown over the fence. There was more blood on the ground at the rear of some houses. He met an Indian and asked why there was so much blood around.

"We killed cattle today," was the reply.

Barber accepted this explanation, and after a short time met Eneas George.

"You'll have to come to the lockup with me, Eneas," he said. "I'll have to arrest you for stabbing your wife."

Eneas grinned foolishly and said he was sorry. Barber then made inquiries about Carr and Gisbourne. He was told that they had been at the reserve but went away. On the way back to Merritt, Barber asked Eneas about the officers.

"They came last night and went away again. I was not there. It was what somebody told me."

"Did you hear where they were going?"

"No, they just went away."

This story tallied with the others that Barber had picked up. He surmised that the Constables had given chase to cattle thieves or bootleggers, and their return was only a matter of hours. After locking Eneas up he went home.

There is no telling how long the Constables' disappearance would have remained a mystery had a commercial traveller not been driving along the road towards Merritt. He came to a turn where a signpost marked "Petit Creek" pointed to a bridge over the Nicola River to the Canford Reserve. He slowed cautiously as he neared the outer edge of the road, and just north of the bridge saw a Ford V8, its back against a tree. Only the tree prevented the vehicle from toppling into the swirling waters of the Nicola River. The traveller stopped and got out.

On his way to the car, he was undecided about whether to report it. The police, he thought, probably knew all about it — just another case of a drunken party where gasoline and liquor didn't mix. Accidents like these were all too common with high-speed cars on mountain roads.

The car's windshield, the traveller noted, was splintered, and there was a large pool of blood on the running board. The interior was soaked in blood: the seats, the floor, the door panels, even the windows were splashed. A pair of handcuffs and a police baton lay on the front seat. An Oxford shoe was on the running board.

On his way to Merritt, he thought once more about reporting the wreck to the police. So far as he could see, judging from the baton and hand-cuffs, they knew about it. There would be little sense in telling them what they already knew. Besides, they might hold him for questioning. He decided to say nothing about it and began calling on his customers.

In the meantime, a search was being conducted for the missing officers.

Detective Sergeant W.A. MacBrayne, left, and Sergeant W.J. Service at the Canford Reserve during the investigation. Sergeant Service was later murdered in Prince Rupert.

No one, so far as the investigators could learn, had heard of them.

In Merritt the commercial traveller mentioned the wrecked car to one of his customers. The merchant, aware that a search was being conducted for the two Constables, was extremely interested. He asked for further details. The traveller described the car and its licence number. He was going to say more when a small girl gasped and ran from the store. The traveller turned.

"Who is that little girl?" he asked, astonished.

"The Indian Agent's daughter. It was the Indian Department car that you saw. Something terrible has happened."

Indian Agent Barber listened to his daughter's story. There could be no mistaking her vivid description of the car. He left at once for the scene and raced down the embankment. One glance and he suspected the worst. It was his official car. But where were the Constables?

Barber was shocked by his examination of the vehicle. He noted the baton and recognized the shoe as Gisbourne's. The handcuffs, too. They were ominous. If there had been a fight the officers would have been heard from by now. But the amount of blood within the car and on the running board indicated more than a fight. The scene suggested nothing less than ruthless slaughter.

Barber immediately reported the discovery to Provincial Police Divisional Headquarters at Kamloops. Staff Sergeant W.J. Service and Constable Carmichael left at once for their 70-mile (112-km) trip to Merritt.

Service made a few inquiries and advised Inspector Shirras at Kamloops that he felt that both Constables had been murdered. The Inspector notified headquarters at Victoria and experts were sent. They included Detective Sergeant MacBrayne and Staff Sergeant Peachey of the Criminal Investigation Branch. Together with the other officers, including Inspector Shirras, they went to Canford Reserve.

The bloodstains at the reserve didn't fool the officers. They knew that Indians didn't kill their cattle in such a sloppy manner. They then went to Chief Billy's house where they found Joseph George, his head wrapped in bandages.

"How did you hurt your head?" he was asked.

A blank stare from the injured man was the only answer.

"A horse kicked his head," somebody offered.

"When?"

There was no reply, but inquiry showed that Joseph George had been uninjured prior to the night of May 23.

More questions were asked, and as they talked the officers were closely examining every person in the room. Richardson George attracted the most attention. There was something odd about him — nothing very definite, but enough to arouse curiosity.

Richardson George glared at the police. He had never been in trouble with the law, but he had never tried to avoid it.

"Are those your regular clothes?" he was suddenly asked.

Richardson said they were. The officers were not convinced. His clothes, though worn, were not as ragged as usual. They looked as if they had been recently donned. Further questioning failed to make Richardson tell anything about his sudden change in clothing. He did, however, admit to having changed clothes.

Richardson vigorously denied having seen Carr or Gisbourne. He said they had been at the reserve, but went away. Despite his denials, he was placed under arrest.

Joseph George was practically unconscious. Plainly he was suffering and needed medical attention. But no one as yet came forward to tell how Joseph was injured.

Alex George was not at the reserve. However, the officers took Richardson and Joseph along with them. Joseph was placed in hospital under police guard while Richardson was locked up.

By now the police were certain that the four George brothers — Eneas, Richardson, Joseph and Alex — had killed the two Constables at the reserve on the night of May 23. Bits of information came to them which practically outlined what had taken place on that fatal night. It was a horrifying story.

When it was learned that the police had suspects locked in the cells, loose talk around Merritt suggested that the two officers might purposely have disappeared. Though not believing in it, the investigators checked on all known facts regarding Carr and Gisbourne.

A searching inquiry proved that Constable Percy Carr's history and official conduct were above reproach. A considerate man, devoted to his family, he had been a respected and trusted officer of more than seventeen years' experience. The Indians of Canford Reserve considered him their best friend. Not a single critical voice had ever been raised against him in the district.

On checking Gisbourne's record it was found that he was not greatly experienced in handling Indians. Yet he regarded their welfare as his trust and was merciless to white liquor pedlars who sold their rotgut to the natives. On several occasions, Gisbourne had found Indians in Merritt under the influence of liquor. He had driven them home and advised them to stay sober in the future. On other occasions he had taken Indians from the city lockup and delivered them to their homes.

There was not the slightest reason for either officer to vanish.

Continuing the investigation, Staff Sergeant Peachey went over the wrecked car in search of fingerprints. His search was unsuccessful. The lack of prints could be accounted for by a culprit's fingers being dirty and dust covered. Moisture from the fingers would have been absorbed by the dust and prevented a print.

Other officers were carrying exhibits to the Merritt courthouse. They ranged from sticks to heavy pieces of timber, all splashed with blood stains.

One puzzling aspect of the crime was a tree stump a short distance from the road leading from the gates of the reserve. The marks of an automobile were visible and indicated that the tree has been pulled to one side. Why, officers wondered, should a car leave the road and become entangled with a tree so that it seemed necessary to saw the tree down?

By now officers had two stories about events on the night of May 23. Both were fundamentally the same, both were shocking — even to veteran officers accustomed to gruesome murder cases.

Details uncovered by the investigating officers indicated that Carr and Gisbourne had not expected trouble as they drove to the reserve and stopped in front of Chief Billy's house. Gisbourne went to arrest Eneas George for stabbing his wife while Carr remained in the car.

On rounding the corner of Chief Billy's house, Gisbourne met the four George brothers. They were truculent and appeared under the influence of liquor. Gisbourne asked Eneas to accompany him. Eneas refused and made some insulting remark. Gisbourne reached to grasp him and Eneas struck back. Then like the quick heat of a forest fire, rage spread through the brothers.

They went berserk, attacking Gisbourne with savage fury. Gisbourne backed away. He drew a small .25-calibre automatic pistol from his pocket and fired a shot just as Joseph George charged in. The explosion seemed to deafen Joseph, who staggered back clutching his head. Richardson George, now armed with a stick, yelled that Gisbourne had killed his brother and must be killed in turn. Gisbourne, now thoroughly aware that he was fighting for his life, aimed his pistol and pulled the trigger. The gun did not fire.

Like an avenging fury the brothers were on him. His only weapon was a long flashlight. Using this as a club he tried to fight off the brothers who were wielding their sticks with telling effect. Showers of blows smashed down on him. Blood poured from a dozen wounds in his head. Gisbourne fought furiously, but his attackers kept him off with their long sticks and soon the blows were falling faster on the rapidly weakening officer.

At the sound of the shot, Constable Carr leaped from the car and ran towards the fight just in time to see Gisbourne go down. On seeing the of-

The abandoned police car, blood stains on the seats and running board.

ficer, Richardson George shouted: "Here is the other policeman. Kill him, kill him! Hit him, murder him!"

Unarmed, Carr faced the murderous attack. His fists crashed home time and time again, but they were no match for the heavy sticks that were hitting him from all angles. Realizing that he was fighting a losing battle, the gallant Constable retreated towards the gate.

The Indians pursued, their sticks battering down Carr's fast waning resistance. He staggered from a hard blow. Another one landed on him and his hands dropped. Carr sank to the ground.

Maddened beyond reason, the brothers picked up pieces of railroad ties near the gate and battered the unconscious Carr. Satisfied that he was dead they took Joseph to Chief Billy's house.

Chief Billy was badly frightened. He knew the George brothers were now in a serious plight and he wished to keep out of it. They, however, warned him to say nothing to anyone. They also warned the other Indians that they would be killed if they said anything to the police. Then they set about disposing of the officers' bodies.

Unable to drive, Eneas, Richardson and Alex forced another Indian to act as chauffeur. Gisbourne's body was thrown on to the rear seat and searched. They found $30 which they divided. Carr's body joined Gisbourne's and the trio then climbed into the car.

Their unwilling driver took the car off the reserve and was heading along the road when Constable Carr emitted a loud groan. This sound so unnerved him that he lost control of the vehicle and crashed into a tree. Furious, the George brothers jumped out, grabbed some rocks and battered Carr's head to a bloody mass. Then they ordered their driver to get going.

But the car was jammed against the tree. The brothers returned to the reserve for an axe and saw and cut the tree down. Then they got a horse and hauled the car onto the road.

The driver was terrified. Too upset to drive properly, he left the choke open and careened along the road. About 200 yards (180 m) from the highway bridge the car rolled backwards down the embankment. Here it came to rest against a tree close to the river.

The George brothers took the bodies of the unfortunate officers and threw them into the Nicola River. Gisbourne's body floated away, but Carr's battered remains clung to the shore until Eneas George pushed it into the current. The killers returned to the reserve. Here Richardson, whose clothing was well stained with the blood of the murdered men, changed and buried the incriminating evidence.

That, in substance, was what happened on that fateful night. The George brothers were ordered to stand trial in Vernon.

As soon as the facts were known the public split into factions. What had been a case of brutal murder speedily became a controversial trial. Interest in the case became extreme. On the day of the trial hundreds sought admittance to the courtroom. They came in business suits and range garb to join Indians from various reserves.

Stuart Henderson, a seventy-one-year-old veteran, assisted by Henry Castillou, appeared for the defence. Before the trial was fairly under way, the defence lawyer suggested that the killings were justifiable homicide on the grounds that neither Carr nor Gisbourne had a warrant, or the legal right to arrest Eneas George under the circumstances. He skillfully evaded the fact that an officer does not require a warrant to arrest a person charged with assault with intent to kill or do bodily harm.

With such legal luminarys battling for their rights, the George brothers found themselves lionized by misguided sympathizers who actually believed that they had killed to save their own lives. Joseph George, still suffering from the gunshot explosion, was not present and became an object of acute sympathy.

This ridiculous attitude on the part of people who should have known better placed the case in a position far out of keeping with its actual importance. One enthusiast, who, if he had been pinned down to hard realism would have cheerfully admitted that he didn't care what happened to the Indians, dug up an ancient charter. It rambled aimlessly to the effect that Indians were to be left alone on their own reservations no matter what happened, so long as it happened on their reserve. According to this charter, he said, the police had no right to arrest these poor, innocent children.

As the trial proceeded it became evident that three brothers had stood by a fourth to prevent his being taken into custody for the crime of stabbing his wife. Had he been the picture of meek innocence, so ably painted by his astute lawyers, Eneas George would have gone with Gisbourne. Instead, he chose murder. His brothers aided him and were therefore equally guilty. It was also said that the George brothers hated Gisbourne for his vigorous prosecution of liquor pedlars. Stuart Henderson made an impassioned plea for acquittal, but the jury found the three George brothers guilty of murder. The judge pronounced the death sentence.

But the fight for the lives of the George brothers had only started. An appeal was launched. It was allowed and a new trial ordered.

Joseph George's case was beginning to present some difficulties and points of law. He was stone deaf. Therefore, he could not be tried until his hearing was restored or a practical means of communicating was devised. He could neither read nor write English. So long as Joseph George remained mute and refused to co-operate he was beyond the law of the criminal court.

For almost seventeen months a legal battle raged around the George brothers. Their trials cost the British Columbia government more than $30,000.

Eloquent counsel described the prisoners and their characters with such flowery rhetoric that one momentarily expected them to step from the prisoner's dock clad in white robes and halos. They ignored the irrefutable evidence which described the actions of these prisoners on that May night. Other people felt pity for the poor innocent Indians and attempted to pluck a symphony of compassion on the heartstrings of the nation. But not one word was raised for the widows and fatherless children of the murdered Constables. Despite fierce opposition, the Crown succeeded in sustaining the death penalties against Eneas, Richardson and Alex George.

By now Joseph George's hearing had been restored and he was ready for trial. Witnesses swore that Joseph George, after the first blows were struck, was rendered helpless and took no further part in the fight. The jury acquitted him.

Constable Carr's body was recovered from the Fraser River at Cheam View in the Fraser Valley. It was identified by war wounds, and had been in the water for two months, floating down the Nicola into the Thompson and the Fraser to be picked up 280 miles (450 km) downstream.

The three brothers awaited execution in Oakalla Prison. Once again the zealots had a field day. They circulated petitions asking the Minister of Justice to spare the condemned men. After a review, the Minister did commute Alex George's sentence to life imprisonment. But he refused to intervene with Eneas and Richardson George.

On the morning of November 6, 1936, they walked silently to the gallows. Joining them was a white man, Charles Russell, a husky young Vancouver hood who considered himself above the law. The hangman's noose around his neck proved him wrong. His story is told in the next chapter.

Criminal gangs were comparatively rare in Western Canada.
One exception was in Vancouver in 1935 when the Hyslop gang
embarked on a trigger-happy spree that resulted in

Two 20-Year Sentences, Two Bullets, and Two Ropes for the Six.

The bank where teller Hobbs was murdered, setting off the most intensive manhunt in Vancouver's history.

It began amateurishly on December 18, 1935, when two of them tried to hold up Spurgeon's Jewelry Store in New Westminster. Scared off by a clerk's screams, they had a running gun fight with Constable Dan Gunn, then their getaway car struck a street car and, seconds later, a milk truck. They abandoned the car to escape on foot.

Less than a week later on December 23 the same two men and a freckled, red-haired companion walked, gun in hand, into the Royal Bank on Vancouver's Commercial Drive. They roughed up the manager when he attempted to resist and scooped up $3,000.

They had come by a taxi which circled the block and picked them up. In the back was driver Bill Perry, bound and gagged with adhesive tape. Twenty minutes later he was found in the abandoned cab. He said four men had hired him to go to Stanley Park. In a secluded spot at gun point they tied him up and bundled him on the floor. The man who took over the wheel wore horn-rimmed glasses.

Hastily summoned police ploughed through descriptions and finally identified James Lawler and Dave Anderson, the same pair who attempted to hold up Spurgeon's Jewelry Store. The man with the red hair and freckles was Jack "Red" Hyslop. Nothing further developed through Christmas, except for an underworld rumor that Lawler and Anderson had left town.

Three weeks later a taxi deposited three men outside the Bank of Commerce at Powell Street and Victoria Drive. With guns drawn the trio moved into the bank and started shooting. The first bullet struck teller W.H. Hobbs in the throat. He swayed for a second then fell to the floor. Manager Tom Winsby courageously pulled his automatic and fired at the robbers but a bullet struck his arm. Then one of the gangsters stepped across the blood-drenched Hobbs to clean the cash drawer of $1,200.

Money in a paper bag, guns in hand, the three men left. With split second timing, their block-circling cab stopped in front of them. Coolly the red-haired gang leader pocketed his gun. He pulled out a packet of cigarettes, lit one, and handed the pack to a companion. Just then he noticed a crowd gathering in the doorway of a nearby beer parlor. He yanked out his gun and the sightseers wisely vanished.

As the cab sped down Powell Street it was followed by a passing

Chuck Russell — he shot the teller and the manager.

Earl Dunbar — he drove the gang's vehicle.

motorist to the 800 block Clark Drive where he saw the gunmen jump out and race round a corner. Promptly he phoned the police. As fast as the radio squad cars were on the scene, the bandits were faster. They'd regained their own car and vanished.

While police cars scoured the neighborhood and detectives took notes in the bank, there came an excited call from a man who identified himself as taxi-cab driver D.R. Warnock. He had picked up three men who wanted to visit Stanley Park. Once there they had stuck him up with a gun, bound and gagged him with adhesive tape, and thrown him in the bushes.

Witnesses checking Criminal Investigation Branch mug books were positive the red-haired Hyslop had participated in both robberies, but with different companions. This time his accomplices turned out to be Jack "Blackie" Lawson and Charles "Chuck" Russell. There was no clue as to the driver of the cab who on both occasions had worn horn-rimmed glasses.

Teller Hobbs was rushed to hospital with a bullet in his spine. He died the next morning, a callous killing that shocked Vancouver citizens. Chief of Police W.W. Foster immediately summoned his bureau heads for a conference that had one objective: maximum effort to catch the killers.

The first break came from a woman living on East 8th Avenue. When she heard the evening news of the robbery, she remembered that a car had stopped in a nearby lane after lunch. Two men had walked toward 9th Avenue and the car was still there.

Detectives George Lefler and Frank White promptly checked the vehicle. The key was still in the ignition, the owner registered as Donald McNeill. On returning to headquarters they learned that McNeill had just reported his car as stolen. It was 7 p.m.

They visited McNeill and noticed that he seemed uneasy. He left the car, he said, outside his house that morning and missed it around 2:30 p.m. Why he had taken so long to inform the police he couldn't explain.

"Did you leave the key in the ignition?" asked Lefler.

"Of course not!" came the indignant reply.

"Funny. It was in when we found it," was Lefler's reply. "How about telling us the real story?"

McNeill admitted he had some friends on East 10th who wanted the use of the car on December 15, the day of the bank robbery, and he'd agreed to leave it in front of his house. When he came at 2:30 he noticed the car wasn't back and went to see them. They told him they'd had "a tough break."

"Tough break?"

"Yes, they... well... they said the car was hot," came the explanation.

According to McNeill, when he read in the evening paper of the bank shooting he felt he'd better report his car as stolen. The detectives took him to headquarters to see if anything further occurred to him.

As Lefler was reporting to CID Inspector Gordon Grant, there came a phone report that the driver of the getaway taxi in both bank robberies had been identified and his address discovered. He was Earl Dunbar, holder of a seventeen-year criminal record.

The police went to his address only to find him gone. But there were other things there: a gun, mask and a picture postcard. It was from a western U.S. city and gave a cryptic clue to the whereabouts of the missing Lawler and Anderson who had taken part in the jewelry store and Royal Bank robberies. Vancouver police promptly contacted by phone and telegram one U.S. city after another. But the fugitives seemed always one day ahead of their enquiries.

In the meantime the men on East 10th who had borrowed McNeill's car had not been overlooked. It was barely twenty-four hours since the bloody raid on the bank, and twelve hours since the death of young Hobbs when squad cars converged on the house. Chief Foster led the policemen, among them Superintendent Harold Darling and Detective Inspector Gordon Grant.

No lights were showing when Darling and Grant rang the bell. There was silence, but the door opened a crack. Grant and Darling hurled themselves into the hall, Grant's gun pressing into the doorman's stomach.

"Not a sound," he said in low tones. "Just lead the way."

Behind the living room door was Earl Dunbar who, seeing Grant's gun, hoisted his hands. He was found to be weaponless. From under a bed police hauled "Chuck" Russell. He was relieved of two guns, a 32.20 and a .32, as well as a roll of surgical tape — the kind used to gag taxi drivers.

The man who opened the door said he was Walter Davis, "Just a visiting friend."

There was plenty of food and money in the house, and judging by the hundreds of cigarette butts, there had been many hours of nervous discussion. An important find was a revolver stolen from the Royal Bank in December. Russell and Dunbar were booked for murder; Davis as an accessory.

Next day Dunbar was positively identified as the one who drove the getaway taxis. The man with the horn-rimmed glasses was Russell, a fashion-conscious young hood. He was identified as the man who killed teller Hobbs. If further proof was needed, the police laboratory supplied it — his 32.20 revolver had fired the fatal shot.

One man connected with the 10th Avenue dwelling the police would have been glad to see was the landlord, Fred Healey. It was he who'd furnished the sanctuary after the shooting. He hadn't returned to 10th Avenue where detectives still kept a chilly vigil, and although he was an intimate of Earl Dunbar, he hadn't turned up at his address. Finally, Healey settled the matter. He gave himself up and was booked as an accessory.

With two of the gang under arrest and two being trailed in the States, Vancouver police had reason to be satisfied with their progress a day after the robbery. But there were still two men missing — Hyslop and Lawson. Day and night the intensive search went on, men ignoring their off-duty time to work twelve and fifteen hour days. On Monday, January 20, nearly a week after the Powell Street bank robbery, Detective Grant had only nine hours' sleep in five days.

Persistent questioning revealed that Hyslop and Lawson had been at the East 10th Avenue house where Dunbar and Russell were arrested but had left with two women before the police raid. Descriptions of the women were soon in every officer's notebook. Constables J. Mathieson and J.

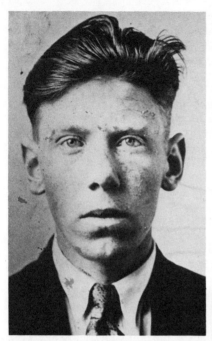

Freckle-faced Red Hyslop, the gang leader, and Blackie Lawson shot themselves rather than face trial and probable hanging.

New Westminster as it looked when the gang began its shooting spree.

Wastall, beat men in the city's West End, decided that a woman known as Maxwell bore a resemblance to one of the two.

Soon detectives were knocking at the door. Getting no answer, they entered on a pass key. Mrs. Maxwell had some interesting items in her bureau drawer, including the missing Blackie Lawson's birth certificate, letters addressed to her from the States, a box of fifty .32 calibre shells, and thirty-four 32.20 shells. Checking with neighbors, the officers discoverd that Mrs. Maxwell had left hurriedly with a girl friend three days before. The detectives, except for one, departed.

Around mid-afternoon he heard the sound of a key in the lock, and stood to greet a flashily dressed woman in her late twenties. When she recovered from her surprise she admitted she was Mrs. Maxwell. Later she said she was Frances Edwards and finally agreed her name was Frances Morton. She knew Lawson and Hyslop but hadn't seen them lately. Morton was taken to headquarters and jailed.

About nine o'clock that evening, the detective was again disturbed. This time by a chunky little blonde, Morton's girl friend, Mary Gorry. She, too, admitted knowing the wanted men but hadn't seen them in weeks. Gorry joined Frances Morton in the lockup.

Although police kept the women's room and the two other premises staked out, there was no sign of the wanted pair. Pressure was applied to the underworld but all police could learn was that the killers were still in town. But as a result of the pressure, seven days after the Powell Street holdup came a tip. The fugitives, breathed an informer, were going to move from a secret hideout to a new location — the Oaks Rooms on East Hastings. They'd be there after eight that evening.

That night Chief Foster and Superintendent Darling led a twenty-man squad to the address. They took up positions around the building, all knowing one thing: they were dealing with two desperate men who were going to shoot it out. They were men who knew that if they were arrested they would hang.

Inside the building in a sparsely furnished room on the second story at the end of the corridor were the two hunted men — twenty-three-year-old Jack Hyslop, the red-haired and freckle-faced gang leader, and thirty-year-old Blackie Lawson. Elsewhere in the city they'd been cooped up for 168 hours in a hideout; hours of chain smoking, planning, arguing; hours filled with fear and foreboding. From radio newscasts they were continually reminded that they were the focus of the greatest manhunt in Vancouver's history.

When they decided to change hideouts, one of them had used the phone. It was then some criminal "friend," Judas-like and anxious for police favor, had passed the word. They had their guns, but only ten rounds of ammunition. They could get no more; they were too "hot." Like two tarred rats in a cellar, the other rats shunned them. Not from moral scruples, but from fear of being jailed for helping two men wanted for murder.

So the pair had slipped furtively after dark into the Oaks Rooms and now behind its locked door were smoking and debating their next move. Perhaps it was Hyslop who went over to the window and drew the curtain back. Maybe he saw under the downpour outside figures on the glistening sidewalk, or possibly spotted the occasional flicker of a police flashlight at the side of the building.

Maybe it was the incessant barking of an Alsatian dog chained in an open woodshed in the nearby alley that gave them alarm. It barked because just out of its reach sat Detective Alan Hoare on a box, gun in hand, watching the foot of a long, wooden fire-escape.

About 8:30 rookie Detective Archie Plummer began checking the register on the second floor. As he thumbed through its greasy pages in the ill-lit hallway, Detective Sergeant Hann tiptoed past, heading for the stairs at the end of the hall.

Around them were the usual sounds of a rooming-house — the clatter of dishes, the moving of a chair, muted laughter. As Hann mounted the first step there was another sound — two muffled pistol shots. They signalled an extraordinary turn to the case.

Hann raced in the direction of the shots, passing tenants at their doors. "In there," one nodded towards Room 40. Next moment, gun in hand, Hann was pounding on the door.

"Open up in there. Police!" was his command. But there was only silence. Other detectives joined Hann who waited no longer but crashed the door open.

The room was dark and filled with acrid fumes of powder. The fugitives lay on the floor, their bodies at right angles, feet almost touching. Apparently they had stood facing one another in their last second of life, and both had fired a bullet through his left temple. They must have fired in unison. Hyslop's hand grasped his .38 Smith & Wesson, and near Lawson's hand lay his .38 Iver Johnson.

On the bed was the tan snap brim hat that Hyslop had worn when he robbed the Bank of Commerce on Powell Street; near it was a pair of horn-rimmed glasses — probably those used by Dunbar when driving the getaway cabs. Of the $4,300 the gang had stolen, all that was found was $136.

At an inquest, Hyslop and Lawson were identified as two of the men in the Powell Street bank holdup when Hobbs was murdered. Hyslop was also identified as one of the men in the Royal Bank holdup in December.

Three days after the inquest came word of the last two gang members: Jimmie Lawler and Dave Anderson. The CID had traced them from city to city until it was deduced they were heading for Chicago. Subsequently, when Lawler stepped up to a Chicago post office wicket to ask for a letter, a police gun was thrust in his back.

He led detectives to the hotel suite where a burly sergeant went in ahead to grab Davidson before he could reach a gun. Chief Foster's wire had said "Armed, may be dangerous." It was sound advice. A loaded gun was on the table and another in a dresser drawer.

By the end of the week, both men were back in Vancouver to stand trial for the attempted armed robbery of Spurgeon's Jewelry, for shooting with intent at a New Westminster policeman, and for participating in the Royal Bank robbery in Vancouver.

Before they came to trial Dunbar and Russell were engaged in their fight for life in Vancouver Assize Court. Confederates in crime, they turned out to be enemies at law. In the shadow of the gallows, gang comradeship quickly dissipates.

At their April 1936 trial the tragic story of the shooting of bank teller Hobbs was outlined. L.P. Gordy, a longshoreman, testified that he watched the gunman come out, saw Russell pocket his gun, light a cigarette and pass the pack to a companion before stepping into the cab driven by Dunbar.

Finally, Russell and Dunbar each took the stand. Dunbar said that he drove the getaway cars in two bank robberies under the threat of a gun held by Hyslop, backed up by Lawson and Russell. He couldn't do anything but comply.

Chuck Russell flatly denied being in the bank at the time of the robbery. He said he had got up late that morning. He went out shopping, returning to the house about 12:30 p.m. just in time to hear the news broadcast about a bank robbery. To those in court, the well-dressed Russell gave the impression of being self-possessed and a man with a quick mind.

In his summation to the jury, Chief Justice Aulay Morrison remarked that his alibi was more suggested than proved, and of Dunbar's defence he said: "Compulsion is not a defence unless the compulsion is of such a nature as to make the accused a mere physical instrument." The jury was out an hour, to return with a verdict of "guilty." Russell and Dunbar were sentenced to death.

Fred Healey, the man who had given sanctuary to the gang after the murder, was found guilty of being an accessory after the fact. Chief Justice Morrison apparently found Healey's action so repugnant that he gave him fifteen years.

Finally, there was Walter Davis, the man who had opened the door of the 10th Avenue house the night of the police raid — the man who "was visiting a friend." He, too, had been charged as an accessory, but the Crown withdrew the charge for lack of evidence. The two women were also released.

Lawler and Anderson, brought back from their Chicago jaunt, each got ten years for their part in the pre-Christmas raid on the Royal Bank. A month later they appeared at the New Westminster Assize, and were given another ten years for their attempted armed robbery of Spurgeon's Jewelry Store. A youth named Godbold, driver of their getaway car, kept them company with a ten-year sentence.

At 6:45 a.m. in the rain-laden chill of November 6, 1936, Charles Russell was taken from his Oakalla cell to the scaffold, Salvation Army Major T.S. Stewart beside him. When Russell dropped from sight, Stewart looked at the taughtened rope and remarked: "His soul is in Heaven. He was a fine boy." This sentiment wasn't shared by relatives of the young bank teller so ruthlessly murdered.

On November 27, Major Stewart accompanied Earl Dunbar to his rendezvous with Canada's hangman.

Dunbar was the fifth man to die, ending the bloodstained career of the Hyslop gang. They were all young men who had started out as car stealing kids. They all chose to be done with life by the time they were thirty — two 20-year sentences, two bullets, and two ropes!

Earle Leonard Nelson and one of his
twenty-seven known victims.

148

The Strangler Who Terrified the Prairies

"Nothing in the history of crime known on this continent seemingly parallels the number of his killings or the atrocious acts he ... committed."
Bulletin from the City of Winnipeg Police Department.

On June 8, 1927, a man of about thirty with a dark complexion and piercing black eyes knocked on the door of a rooming house on Smith Street in Winnipeg. It was opened by Katherine Hill, the seventy-year-old landlady. The man said he was answering the room-for-rent sign in the window. Mrs. Hill, a staunch Pentecostal, made it clear that she would tolerate no liquor in the house, nor girls in his room.

"Oh, no," he said. "I wouldn't think of anything like that. I am a religious man."

The room rent was $12 a month, one week in advance. He gave her $1, promising the other $2 the following day. Mrs. Hill agreed and led him to a second floor bedroom where they sat for sometime discussing religion. Later, Mrs. Hill recalled that she firmly believed she had a "decent young man" in the house.

Had Mrs. Hill known the truth about the "decent young man," she would undoubtedly have preferred the devil for a roomer. The name he had given her, Woodcots, was one of twenty-four aliases. His real name was Earle Leonard Nelson and he was wanted in the U.S. for the documented murder of twenty-five women and a baby, and attacks on scores of other women. His motive was rape.

Nelson's horrifying murder record began in Philadelphia on the afternoon of October 18, 1925, with the murder-rape of Olla McCoy. Nineteen days later he strangled May Murray. Both victims had their wrists bound by strips of cloth tied with a complicated knot; both had "room-for-rent" signs in their windows; both had been raped.

Less than a week later Lillian Weiner returned home from school and discovered the body of her mother lying across the bed. The knots in the cloth strips binding her hands were similar to those used in the first two sex murders. In the window was a sign advertising a room-for-rent. She had been raped.

From Philadelphia the killer headed west to San Francisco, his arrival announced by the discovery of the body of Clara M. Newman, a sixty-year-old woman who operated a rooming house. There were finger bruises on her neck and nose, and she had been garrotted by a thin cord. She, too, had been raped.

Then from San Jose came news that a sixty-five-year-old woman had been strangled. She bore similar bruises on her neck. The next victim horrified even hardened police officers. She was sixty-three-year-old Mrs. L. St. Mary who was found dead in her rooming house. The doctor who conducted the autopsy reported that nine of the elderly woman's ribs had been broken in her struggle for life.

By now police had a full description and a series of fingerprints of the man who they believed was the killer. Although he murdered in daylight, he seemed able to disappear after each attack. The *San Francisco Chronicle* referred to him as "The Dark Slayer," a name that would soon be changed to "The Dark Strangler."

Over the next few months women were strangled in various California communities. Then in October from Portland, Oregon, came even more dreadful news. Three women were strangled in three days. Each was raped.

The Strangler then returned to California but his first victim was fortunate. She was Mrs. C. Murray, in the last stage of pregnancy. She opened the door of her rooming house to a suave, friendly man of thirty, showed him various rooms and finally returned to a sleeping porch. He asked whether there was a clothes closet. As she turned her back to open the door, he flung one arm around her throat. His free hand fastened with a smothering grip over her mouth and nose.

Mrs. Murray struggled with such desperation that she broke his death grip. As she started to scream, he fled. The next day he murdered and raped fifty-six-year-old Anna Edmunds who had a broken shoulder.

In the following weeks he moved around the country, arriving two days before Christmas at Council Bluffs, Iowa. Here, in contrast to his other killings which were leisurely, he was in a hurry.

At Council Bluffs he responded to a room-for-rent sign. The landlady, Mrs. O.H. Brown, was very perceptive and sensed an air of urgency about her enquirer that was disquieting. When he asked to inspect the basement, her unease turned to suspicion and she asked him to leave. A few minutes later he was at the home of Mrs. John Berard a few doors away where rooms were advertised.

Berard's body was discovered stuffed behind the furnace in her basement. While the crime had the hallmarks of California's Dark Strangler, one uncharacteristic feature of the case was the unusual haste. Some days later the reason become known.

He had arrived at Council Bluffs by hitchhiking from Portland. The driver had stopped at a garage for repairs. While waiting, his passenger had called at the Brown residence — without success — and a short time later at the Berard home. After strangling and raping Mrs. Berard he returned to the garage and resumed his ride.

Following his stopover at Council Bluffs, the swarthy killer with the engaging smile and hands of death continued to hitchhike and arrived in Kansas City on December 24. That day he murdered and raped a twenty-three-year-old mother, probably in front of her six-year-old son. The boy suffered from congenital defects and after the attack had to be hospitalized. He died less than a month later.

On December 27, the Strangler topped even that crime. He called at a boarding house in which Germania Harpin and her baby son lived. Their bodies were discovered behind a locked bedroom door.

Over the following months the killings continued. In Detroit he murdered two women in one house. Even before the bodies were discovered he had moved to Chicago and murdered another woman. After this killing the *Chicago Herald and Examiner* gave him another nickname — the Gorilla Man.

By now he had strangled and raped at least twenty-four women, killed an eight-month-old baby and probably caused the death of the six-year-old boy. In addition, police estimated that he had attempted to murder at least fifty other women. He had been described minutely by over fifty witnesses, some of whom had spent several hours in his company, and he had left identifiable fingerprints at the scene of many of his crimes. Nevertheless, he continued to escape recognition and in daylight slipped away from his crimes unnoticed.

Not knowing where he would strike next, harried police officers could only continue their surveillance and keep landladies and boarding housekeepers on the alert. Neither action had met with success. Unknown to the U.S. police, however, the Dark Strangler had decided to seek a new land — Canada.

By the morning of June 8, 1927, he had hitchhiked to Winnipeg and by afternoon had found Mrs. Hill's rooming house and paid his $1 deposit on the second-floor bedroom.

Next day, the "decent young man" left the house early and was not seen until suppertime. He apologetically informed Mrs. Hill that he had been unable to raise the $2 but hoped to have the money next day. Mrs. Hill, who had long experience with cash-short young men, said she could wait.

That same evening, in a house on a nearby street, fourteen-year-old Lola Cowan was preparing to go out. Her father's income had been severely restricted by a recent operation. To help with finances, Lola sold artificial flowers made by her sister.

The young girl left the house and walked the short distance towards Smith Street. She was last spoken to about 9:30 p.m. by a householder who wanted to know why she was out at such a late hour. She replied that she had to help the family. Minutes later, Lola turned into Smith Street where Mrs. Hill's new roomer had taken up residence. When she did not return that evening, her father began a search.

The next morning while John Cowan was reporting the disappearance of his daughter to the police, William Patterson was saying goodbye to his pretty young wife, Emily, and their two young children. When he arrived home that evening he discovered that his children were with the next door neighbor.

She told him that they had come to her house about two o'clock, saying their mother had "gone away." While she thought it strange that Emily Patterson had not brought the children over, she allowed them to remain.

At nine, Patterson put his children to bed, not yet concerned about his wife's absence. But when she had not returned by eleven o'clock, he became anxious and phoned the police station to enquire about accidents. None had been reported.

Worried, Patterson began to check the house. He noticed his suitcase in the dining room and found that its lock had been broken. Gone was the envelope in which they kept their savings. His wife's absence now took on a sinister aspect.

A religious man, Patterson knelt beside their bed to pray. As he got up his hand brushed the sheet hanging close to the floor. It revealed the sleeve of his wife's dress. She was dead.

In response to Patterson's desperate phone call, the police arrived with Coroner Dr. H. Cameron. He noted that Emily Patterson's face was smeared with blood and that the top of her head was bruised. A few strands of hair, presumably from her assailant's head, were in her hand, while across her body were a pair of pants, a coat and hat. There was evidence that she had been raped. She was seven months pregnant.

A stunned Patterson checked for items missing. In addition to the money, he found that his whipcord suit, his wife's wedding ring and pieces of jewelry were gone.

Meantime, in the discarded clothing under the bed Chief of Detectives George Smith found a newspaper clipping listing a room to let on Langside Street. He at once felt that the Patterson slaying was tied to the "Gorilla Man" stranglings in the States. The killer frequently changed clothes — and stealing Patterson's and leaving his own fitted the known pattern. The front porch brought another confirming fact — there was a room-for-rent sign in one of the windows.

Acting on a hunch, Smith instituted a search of all rooming houses and clothing stores in the city. The shop-to-shop canvass brought the first reward. Detective Sergeant Hoskins located Patterson's stolen suit at Waldman's Second Hand Store. From there the killer had left an easily followed trail. He appeared to have been in no hurry, dropping into a smoke shop for cigars and spending an hour in the Central Barber Shop. He was talkative until the barber commented on some fresh scratches on his head. Then the man got agitated and ordered him not to touch him. He left the barber's, purchased a hat at Chevrier's Department Store and boarded a street car.

When a couple who boarded the street car did not have the correct change, the Strangler obligingly provided it for them. He introduced himself as Walter Woods and began discussing religion with them. But they soon discovered they were on the wrong street car. When they got off, he joined them and within minutes they got a ride to their destination of Headingley

18 miles (28 km) to the west. Here, the Strangler parted company with the couple and hitchhiked to Portage la Prairie. Then his trail vanished. He had been in Canada less than two days.

But as a result of his leisurely pace and many visits to various business places, Detective Smith was able to circulate to radio and newspapers a detailed description of him. In addition, detectives checked all rooming houses for anyone suspicious and warned owners about the strangler and his methods. To Detective Kilcup fell the task of calling at Mrs. Hill's rooming house where Woodcots had paid his $1 deposit. No one there connected the "decent young man" with the Dark Strangler — or the now three-day missing teenager, Lola Cowan.

On Sunday afternoon, Mrs. Hill looked into Woodcots' room and noted that it was empty. Because she had not seen him since Friday, she suspected that he would not be returning. Leaving the bedroom door open, she went down to discuss the missing boarder with her husband. As a result, Hill phoned the police station and talked to George Smith.

While Smith was talking with Hill, Detective Kilcup returned to the station. Smith directed him to check on the Smith Street rooming house. Kilcup said that he had just come from there. Everything had been normal.

Smith, however, was suspicious. He gave Kilcup the clothing the killer had left at the Patterson residence and told him to see if anyone at the Hill's rooming house could identify it. Kilcup wearily retraced his steps.

In the meantime Bernhardt Mortenson, a resident at the Hill's, went up to his room. As he climbed the stairs he happened to look into Woodcots' room. Something white between the bed cover and the floor caught his attention. He went into the room and peered under the bed. The "something white" was the nude body of a young woman. The discovery so startled Mortenson that he rushed down the stairs and over to a neighbors to phone police. He had completely forgotten that Mrs. Hill's boarding house had a phone.

Shortly after, Detective Kilcup arrived. Though stunned by what had taken place, the Hill's had no difficulty identifying the clothing in the detective's hand as that worn by Woodcots.

News of the second outrage spread rapidly. Mrs. Cowan was driven to the funeral home but the distraught mother was unable to make a positive identification. About 11 o'clock that evening John Cowan, still searching for his daughter, heard about the murder from a street-car conductor. On arriving at the Hill residence he could learn only that the body had been taken to Thompson Funeral Home. A by-stander, noting his obvious distress, drove him to the mortuary. The body was that of his young daughter.

A post mortem by Dr. W.P. McCowan revealed that the girl had died by strangulation. She had been raped.

Both of Winnipeg's newspapers published special editions on Sunday afternoon and panic swept the city. But it didn't stop in Winnipeg, rapidly spreading eastward to Ontario and westward to Alberta. By Monday there was scarcely a hardware store that had not sold its supply of chain locks, rifles, shotguns and ammunition. Housewives stopped answering the door — even to milkmen and others whom they knew personally. It was the

Manitoba Free Press

WINNIPEG, WEDNESDAY, JUNE 15, 1927

STRANGLER TRACED TO SASKATCHEWA[N]

NO RUSSIAN NOTE POLAND WILL TAKE [ ]URE OF ULTIMATUM

Police Chief Who Failed to Run Down Counterfeiters Found To Be Head of Gang

ASSERTS "STRANGLER" IS MODAL [ ]

SUCCESSFUL IN IRISH ELECTIONS

Man Wanted for Winnipeg Murders Last Seen in Regina on Monda[y]

Established Beyond Doubt, Says Chief Bruton, Wanted Man Was in Regina Monday

Winnipeg Police Officers Satisfied Gorilla Man W[as] One Seen in Regina Over Week End, But A Relaxing Vigorous Search in City and Dis[trict] Suspect Given Ride From Kennay to Ale[x] on Saturday.

Manitoba Free Press

WINNIPEG, THURSDAY, JUNE 16, 1927

STRANGLER CAUGHT AND ESCAPE[S]

[S]PECIAL TRAIN CARRIES OUT POLICE FROM WINNIPE[G]

[ ]POWER WARNING [ ] RUSSIA TO CEASE [ ]PAGANDA POSSIBLE

LINDBERGH'S RECEPTION AT WASHINGTON

Locked Up in Killarney Jail, Picks Lock and Gets Away South Country All Arous[ed]

Arrest Made at Wakopa, Five Miles From Internatio[nal] Boundary, by Provincial Policemen on Informa[tion] Supplied by Farmer at Whose Place Man, Clo[sely] Answering Description of Murderer, Had Stopped a Meal—In Double-locked Cell, Approximately [ ]teen Minutes, When He Picked Lock and Escap[ed] Leaving Boots Behind—Whole Country Aroused

---

Manitoba Free Press

WINNIPEG, FRIDAY, JUNE 17, 1927

[S]TRANGLER POSITIVELY IDENTIFIE[D]

MUCH WANTED MAN RETURNS TO WINNIPEG

Witnesses Connect Man Arrested In Killarney With Murders He[re]

Prisoner is Identified by Portland as Adrain Harris, Wanted There for Murder

Police Confident Chain of Evidence Which Wil[l] to Conviction Is Complete. Recaptured at [ ] ney Just as Police Special Pulled in Yes [ ] Morning. Strangler Is Brought Back to Wi[ ] Takes From Train at Outskirts, and Sm[ ] Back Entrance of Police Station.

For a week Nelson was front page news in Western Canada. The photo above shows the crowd which gathered in Winnipeg to see the "Gorilla Man."

greatest wave of hysteria to wash across the prairies since the massacre of whites by Indians at Frog Lake during the 1885 Riel Rebellion.

In addition, the murders totally dominated the news. Author James H. Gray in his excellent book, *The Roar of the Twenties*, captured the atmosphere when he wrote:

The Strangler "...monopolized the 8-column, front-page headlines of the newspapers from Fort William to Edmonton. This was an era in which the Canadian papers were becoming increasingly preoccupied with everything American, from baseball heroes to movie heroines, from mass murders to union derbies, from lynch mobs to ticker-tape parades. But on the day of the greatest emotional binge in American history, when more than 1,800 tons of ticker tape was showered on Charles A. Lindbergh on his triumphal return to New York from his flight to Paris, the story was buried under a one-column head on page eight of the *Manitoba Free Press*. It devoted its prime front-page space to reportage of the fruitless search for The Strangler, who overnight had become the 'Gorilla Man' of the headline writers."

The Strangler, however, following a pattern familiar to U.S. lawmen, was now far away in Regina. He had arrived on Saturday and selected a room at Mrs. Mary Rowe's boarding house. He gave his name as Harry Harcourt and paid $4 in advance.

At Mrs. Rowe's boarding house he rose early on Sunday morning — the day Lola Cowan's body was discovered — and walked to the New Wonder Cafe for a meal. On returning, he found the door of one of the upstairs rooms open and boldly walked in. Grace Nelson, another boarder, was lying on her bed. Apologizing for his intrusion, he lingered a few moments then left.

In the back garden he found twelve-year-old Jessie Rowe. After talking with her for a few minutes they left the yard together. Sometime later the girl's mother went in search of her daughter. She found Jessie returning from the cafe where the new boarder had bought her an ice-cream.

On Monday morning, he had breakfast at the cafe and bought a newspaper. Back in his room he learned how accurate a description the Winnipeg police had of the Gorilla Man and the clothing he had bought at Waldman's Second Hand Store.

Discarding most of his clothing he made his way to a department store where he purchased a pair of blue overalls, a khaki shirt and a cap. From there, following his established pattern, he stopped at a second-hand store and sold a hat for 50 cents. Unknown to him, a copy of the morning *Regina Leader* which contained the detailed description was lying on the counter.

After he left, the store owner checked the description. Then he saw a Winnipeg trade-mark in the hat band and phoned police.

While Regina police were swinging into action, the suspect was quietly leaving the city. He had no difficulty picking up rides. The third one of the day was with Isidore Silverman, a scrap metal dealer. Giving his name as Virgil Wilson, he spent the rest of the day helping Silverman load his truck as they visited farms and small villages along the way. That night they stayed at a hotel in Arcola in southeastern Saskatchewan. For the Strangler the choice of hotel had a disastrous consequence.

J.M. Grant, an ex-Manitoba provincial policeman who still kept in close touch with his former officers, worked at the hotel. He noticed the name Virgil Wilson in the register. Knowing this name to be an alias of the Gorilla Man, he checked the guest's description with the night clerk. It matched that circulated by Winnipeg City Police. When Grant reported his discovery alerts were sent immediately to all police detachments in southeast Saskatchewan and southern Manitoba, while continuous radio broadcasts warned the public. Police throughout the prairies picked up hundreds of transients for questioning, with one newspaper estimating that 1,000 men eventually were detained.

Meanwhile, the unsuspecting Silverman and his notorious passenger were making their way leisurely across the prairie, stopping the next evening at Deloraine, Manitoba.

The two men left on Wednesday morning and made a few more calls before reaching Boissevain about 10:30. Although police cars constantly passed along the highway between the two Manitoba towns, the frequent diversions Silverman made to call at farmhouses enabled his passenger to escape detection. At Boissevain the two parted, Silverman heading north to Winnipeg.

The first identification of Earle Nelson came later in the afternoon when Roy Armstrong of Boissevain was accosted by a man who stepped boldly in front of his car. Armstrong picked him up, but almost immediately suspected that his rider was the wanted man. After driving a short distance he made the pretext of having to turn off the main highway in order to get rid of his unwanted passenger. He then circled and sped back to alert police.

In Winnipeg, Commissioner Martin of the Manitoba Provincial Police made plans to send a heavy motorcade of police to scour the area, but they were delayed when heavy rains made roads connecting the capital and Boissevain treacherous. Radio broadcasts warned all residents not to pick up hitchhikers and road blocks were established.

The station at Killarney where Nelson was recaptured after his escape.

In the meantime, Nelson had already hitched several short rides and arrived in Wakopa, a small community 5 miles (8 km) from the international border. Shortly before six o'clock, he bought some cheese and soft drinks at Morgan's General Store. Although Nelson was in the store for only a few minutes, Morgan was suspicious and followed him. He encountered Albert Dingwall and motioned him to join. Later they were met by two other men. After a short consultation they decided that Morgan should notify the nearest police detachment while the rest maintained a surveillance.

Morgan contacted Constable W.A. Gray of the Killarney Detachment. Gray located the miniature posse and quickly determined that the wanted man was moving towards the border along the railway tracks. He circled in front of Nelson and hid behind a clump of bushes. As Nelson appeared, Gray accosted him, revolver in hand.

Nelson made no resistance, nor showed surprise at the sudden appearance of the police officer, but quietly accompanied him to the police car. He was taken to Killarney police headquarters and jailed, his shoes taken away as a precautionary measure. Constable Dunn of the town patrol was left in charge of the cell block.

About five minutes after the departure Dunn, anticipating a sleepless night watching the prisoner, left to buy some matches. He later said that he was gone only four minutes. As he entered the front door he heard the back door close. He found the door of Nelson's cell open and the elusive Dark Strangler gone. He peered outside but could see nothing through the heavy rain.

Commissioner Martin in Winnipeg was quickly notified. He made immediate plans to have a special train sent with a posse of Provincial Police. At Killarney, Constable Gray and Sewell formed some 150 men into posses and began a search. But the Dark Strangler had disappeared, although not far.

Early the next morning, Thursday, June 16, while angry posses were combing the surrounding countryside, a woman was frantically phoning Constable Gray. She had seen a man emerge from beneath a freight platform and walk towards the east end of town. Collecting several remaining townsmen, Gray began a search. Aware that the night of fear had town residents in a state of edginess, Gray was anxious to capture the killer before one of the posses overtook him and carried out a hanging.

In the meantime, Nelson had taken temporary refuge beside a grain elevator. But he was a peculiar kind of fugitive. He noticed a man near the elevator and boldly walked out and asked him for the "makings of a cigarette." He ruined the first, but manufactured another and then walked leisurely back to his hideout.

The man, Alfred Wood, not wishing to arouse Nelson's suspicions, waited until he was out of sight before sending two boys to contact Constable Gray. The news that the Dark Strangler had been sighted quickly spread. Even as Constables Gray and Renton sped to the elevators, people began to move towards the place.

Just then, the whistle of the train bringing police reinforcements from Winnipeg sounded on the outskirts of town. On hearing it, Nelson left his hiding place and moved into the open, evidently intending to board the train. But as he walked towards the station, he was seen.

Wood, who had remained close to Nelson's hiding place, was the man closest to the killer. As Nelson turned to flee, Wood threw up his hand and shouted "Stop!" Meekly, the Dark Strangler halted.

At that moment, the car containing Constables Gray and Renton arrived. Nelson was hastily bundled in and taken to the station before the crowd could reach the scene. He then boarded the train, but not in the manner intended. He had been in Canada eight days.

On the journey to Winnipeg Nelson smoked constantly, told jokes and denied any knowledge of the city or the sex-slayings. Only when his police escort left the station and formed a motorcade to the Winnipeg Police Station did he exhibit signs of stress. Alerted that the famous suspect had been captured, a crowd estimated at upwards of 4,000 gathered round the police building. He expressed fear that the crowd might "rough house" him. However, the detectives easily cleared a path through the crowd and entered the prison without incident.

Nelson was charged with the murders of Lola Cowan and Emily Patterson, his trial set for July 26, 1927. The date was later changed to November 1 because Nelson refused a lawyer and the Court had to appoint James H. Stitt who required more time to prepare a defence.

While awaiting trial Nelson was transferred to the provincial jail on Vaughn Street. Because of his ability to escape and for his protection from other prisoners, he was confined in the death cells. By a strange coincidence, he was only a short distance from the house from which young Lola Cowan had set out on the fateful evening of June 9.

Some 400 spectators, most of them women and girls in their teens, crowded round the courtroom doors when they opened at 2 p.m. on November 1. Some, with lunches, had been there since 7:30 that morning. Lawyer Stitt's defence was that Nelson wasn't guilty by reason of insanity. But among forty-eight witnesses presented by the Crown was Dr. A.T. Mathers, psychiatrist at Winnipeg General Hospital. He stated that Nelson was not insane but that his behaviour was basically that of a constitutional psychopath — a person without conscience or guilt.

At the end of the three-day trial, the twelve-man jury took only forty minutes to bring in their verdict — guilty. Nelson was sentenced to hang on Friday, January 13, 1928.

On that morning a large crowd formed outside the prison. Because many had gained vantage points from which they could see the scaffold, heavy planks were erected around it. At 7:41 hangman Arthur Ellis sprang the trap and the Dark Strangler plunged through the opening.

The body was taken to Barker's Funeral Home where some 2,000 people filed past the casket, making it one of the largest funerals in Manitoba's history. Then the Dark Strangler was shipped to relatives in California. He had been in Canada just over seven months.

Police Stories from Heritage House

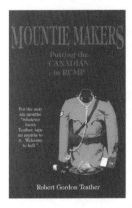 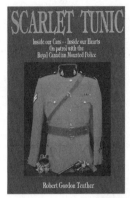 

Robert Teather Trilogy

Mountie Makers	*Scarlet Tunic*	*Scarlet Tunic*
Putting the Canadian	**Inside our Cars…**	**On Patrol with the**
in RCMP	**Inside our Hearts**	**RCMP Vol. 2**
ISBN 1-895811-41-4	**ISBN 1-895811-52-X**	**ISBN 1-895811-01-5**
$14.95	**$11.95**	**$11.95**

  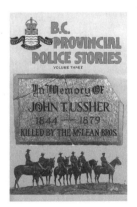

B.C. Provincial Police Stories
Cecil Clark
Vol. 1 • ISBN 1-895811-71-5 • $9.95
Vol. 2 • ISBN 1-894384-29-6 • $9.95
Vol. 3 • ISBN 1-895811-75-9 • $12.95

Heritage House Canadian History

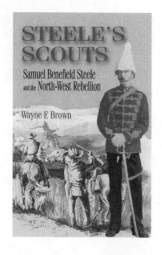

Sitting Bull's Boss
Above the Medicine Line
with James Morrow Walsh
Ian Anderson
ISBN 1-894384-14-8 • $18.95

Steele's Scouts
Samuel Benefield Steele
and the North-West Rebellion
Wayne E. Brown
ISBN 1-895811-63-5 • $17.95

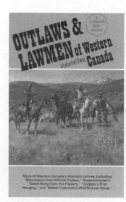

Outlaws & Lawmen
of Western Canada
Vol.1 • ISBN 1-895811-79-1 • $9.95
Vol. 2 • ISBN 1-895811-85-6 • $11.95

March of the
Mounties
ISBN 1-895811-06-6
$12.95